Advance Praise

"Filled with sweet suspense and bitter problems, my dad's book is about his cultural hesitation and how he got over that hesitation. This is a memoir that will be loved for ages and ages."
　　　　—Kristie Wong, nature expert and ten-year-old daughter of Ray Wong

"Seldom have the terms 'self-effacing' and 'memoir' been more faithfully or sweetly conjoined. With his beguilingly humble voice Raymond Wong has shaped a moving, memorable book."
　　　　—Peter Selgin, author of *Confessions of a Left-Handed Man* and *Drowning Lessons*

"Ray Wong's *I'm Not Chinese* is a journey both physical and figurative, a journey from refusal to understanding that sets his feet firmly in two worlds, American and Chinese."
　　　　—Adrian R. Magnuson, author of *Taking Flight*

"Ray Wong's memoir is written with vivid descriptions of place and deep insight into the hearts and minds of the people he meets. You'll visit a cemetery where ancient folklore lives among the graves. You'll taste food and drink described in such detail you'll want to order more of what he likes and spit out what he finds distasteful. For readers who have never been to China, Ray Wong's book will give reason for making the journey."
　　　　—Barbara McMikle, author of *The Secret of the Weeping Monk*

"Raymond Wong's memoir gives readers an insight into the life of a Chinese American who has disowned his Chinese roots. With an honest and open voice, Wong invites readers on his trip to China with his mother, where he learns as much about himself as he does about his mother and her family. It's a touching story not often told and one that readers will find both engaging and thought-provoking. This book made me assess my own relationship with my parents, wondering what important history I have missed because of my own closed eyes."
　　　　—Katherine Pickett, owner of POP Editorial Services and author of *Perfect Bound: How to Navigate the Book Publishing Process Like a Pro*

"Raymond Wong's spare, direct style gets right to the heart of what it means to straddle two cultures. I hope that *I'm Not Chinese* marks the debut of a writer with many more stories to tell."
　　　　—Christine Buckley, Paris-based writer, editor and translator

"In this finely detailed memoir, Raymond Wong takes us on a journey to truths of the heart. Wong travels to China, the country he left as a child. He meets relatives he has never known. At first he holds back. Then slowly his heart opens as his father, aunts, uncles and young cousins embrace him as their own."
　　　　—Glenda Richter, author of *The Stories of Juana Briones: Alta California Pioneer*

"*I'm Not Chinese* is the story of a man who sets out on an international journey to meet the father he never knew, only to find the mother he never quite understood. In a mix of memories and new experiences rendered beautifully to the page, Raymond Wong shows us just what it means to be a family. And in his extended family, we find our own; we see their flaws, discover their fortitude, and reach toward forgiveness. Stunning and resonant, Wong's story is one of acceptance, tenderness, courage, and most of all, unconditional love."

    —Wendy Fontaine

"Raymond Wong's debut memoir *I'm Not Chinese* presents a deeply moving portrayal of the journeys—inner and outer—by which a young man alienated from his family, his ethnicity, and his own feelings discovers a father, reclaims his kin, forgives his mother, and opens his heart to the woman he will marry. With fearless honesty and unusually acute storytelling skills, Wong takes us with him on his eye-opening first encounters with the lives of his Chinese relatives, in opulent restaurants and over-crowded flats in Hong Kong, and in squalid tenements, remote villages, and muddy graveyards in mainland China. Wong not only tells a fast-paced, heartrending story, he offers American readers an arresting glimpse into the realities of contemporary Chinese culture, and the identity dilemmas of thoroughly Americanized children of Asian immigrants."

    —Christine Hale, author of *Basil's Dream, A Novel*

"Raymond Wong's journey escorting his mother on a trip back to Hong Kong is one of discovery of much more than family and culture. *I'm Not Chinese* is a deeply personal portrait full of heart, humor, and compassion."

    —Steve Brannon, Editor, *Small Print Magazine*

"Ray Wong has written a poignant memoir of self-discovery when he accompanies his mother on a trip to China. This episode in his life creates a rare opportunity to find himself on so many different levels: as a son who finally understands his mother's sacrifice and love; as an immigrant to the United States filled with misgivings of his ethnic identity; as a child of a blended family who never found a place to belong; and, as a son who never knew his father. Through interactions with his mother, Wong highlights the difficult choices and perseverance of immigrant mothers. With wry humor and childhood flashbacks, he captures many universal experiences, yet his observations and familial interactions open up a window to the modern Chinese American experience."

    --Susan Hasegawa, Professor of History at San Diego City College

"This is an intimate memoir of Mr. Wong's two journeys: one a physical trip to a fearsome and unknown country and the other an emotional voyage into much darker and more frightening places than mainland China will ever be. The theme of family relationships burns through every page. Old wounds surface; new understanding is reached; and the healing love of re-connections transcends the widest ocean in the world."

    --Elisabeth Newbold, Librarian at the San Diego County Library, Alpine branch

"Raymond Wong's book has defined the aspects of his predicament of shunning his family, ethnicity, and country while taking us on a heart-warming journey from bitterness to clemency, clarity, and respect. It reminds us of all we have in life and to respect and appreciate it with all our heart and soul."

    —Kevin Wong, thirteen-year-old son of Raymond Wong

I'm Not Chinese

The Journey from Resentment to Reverence

Raymond M.Wong

I'm Not Chinese

The Journey from Resentment to Reverence

Raymond M. Wong

Apprentice House

Baltimore, Maryland

First Edition

Printed in the United States of America

Paperback ISBN: 978-1-62720-026-4
Ebook ISBN: 978-1-62720-027-1

Design by Charles Cuthrell
Cover photo by Vina Rathakoune
Edited by Katherine Pickett

Published by Apprentice House

Apprentice House
Loyola University Maryland
4501 N. Charles Street
Baltimore, MD 21210
410.617.5265 • 410.617.2198 (fax)
www.ApprenticeHouse.com
info@ApprenticeHouse.com

For my mother, Kuk Ying Uhlenkamp

Contents

Prologue 序幕... 1

Journey 旅程.. 3

Arrival 抵達... 9

Hong Kong 香港.. 15

Father 父親... 21

Request 要求.. 33

Dwelling 安頓... 41

Survival 生存.. 45

Truth 真相.. 55

Outcasts 孤立... 59

Crossroads 十字路口.. 65

Childhood 童年.. 69

Loyalty 忠誠.. 75

Caring 關懷... 81

Family 家庭.. 87

China 中國... 93

Contrast 對比... 105

Ghosts 鬼...117

Education 教育.. 125

Ancestors 祖先... 133

Commitment 承諾... 141

Wounds 傷口.. 145

Hardship 艱困.. 153

Ingenuity 創造力.. 165

Divided 分裂.. 171

Consequences 後果.. 179

Wall 牆... 185

Hate 恨... 191

Rage 憤怒 199

Connection 投緣 205

Reverence 尊敬 209

Home 家 215

Confession 告白 219

Farewell 告別 223

Epilogue 結語 225

Acknowledgements 227

About the Author 233

Prologue 序幕

The first thing you need to know is I'm not Chinese. My name is Raymond Wong and I stopped being Chinese at the age of five.

Twenty-eight years ago my mother left my father in Hong Kong to come to America in search of a better life. Don't ask about my trip to the US. I don't remember.

What I do know is I'm American. In school, children are cruel to those who are different. Speaking Chinese made me different. I don't speak Chinese anymore.

It's not a big deal. I live in San Diego. My stepfather, Roger, is from Pengilly, Minnesota. Speaking Chinese would only make me an outsider and that's something I've struggled against my whole life. Kids at school used to always ask me what I was. They really wanted to know if I ate with chopsticks.

My answer: British. True. The British government has ruled Hong Kong for over 150 years. My response never failed to bring a puzzled frown and this gave me great satisfaction.

Still no matter how hard I tried, I couldn't fit in—even in my own family. Though I refused to speak Chinese, it didn't bring me closer to the man my mom married when I was six. Roger called me his son, but the words were empty, like a birthday spent alone.

He tried. He really did. It's just something you can't fake.

Either you love someone as your own or you don't. When my brother, Michael, was born, the difference became apparent in the way Roger looked at him.

My sister, Renee, is two years younger than Michael, and almost thirteen years separate us. Michael is close to Roger. Renee has my mother. I've always taken care of myself.

My mom, how do I describe her? A woman who never graduated high school, yet learned to manage property and recently sold a thriving restaurant. Successful, determined, always right. One thing she hasn't been able to do—get my stepfather to quit drinking. But not for lack of effort: fighting, baiting, even blackmail. She hasn't given up.

Her number one goal in life is to get me married, preferably to someone Chinese, so she can show off her grandchildren. Call me stubborn, but this fish isn't biting. The word *marriage* isn't in my vocabulary and being a father is the furthest thing from my mind.

Above all, my mother is a mirror. I see the Chinese reflection and turn away.

So it was with more than a little reservation that I consented to accompany her on a trip to Hong Kong. I'm not sure why I agreed to go. She had asked many times before, but she might as well have spoken in Chinese. This time, a sense of urgency in her voice told me it might be my last chance.

Journey 旅程

Chapter 1

L.A. International, 1996. A delay of the flight to Seoul
en route to Hong Kong stranded us at the terminal, so my
mother and I waited, carry-ons at our feet.

I didn't know what to expect in Hong Kong and only
retained faint impressions of people swarming en masse. My
attitude—try to have no expectations and treat it like any
other vacation. The only problem—spending time with my
mother was anything but relaxing.

I put down the book, *The Courage to Write: How Writers
Transcend Fear*, by Ralph Keyes and looked at my mom. So
strange to see her new hairdo. Prior to the trip, she told me
Hong Kong would be hot in August, but the short hair and
perm came as a complete shock. The length coupled with
the artificial texture made me think of a huge ball of steel
wool atop her head.

I said, "You still haven't told me all the people we're
going to meet in Hong Kong."

"We see many people," my mother replied.

"And my father? When will I get a straight answer about
him?"

She studied the vacant seat across from her, as if
contemplating a matter of great importance. "Something
I never tell you about Hong Kong. When I marry to your
father, I work at cleaning hotels. I was carry you in my
stomach, but I still working. I am hard worker, you know."

She shifted her gaze to me and I nodded. "Late at night, I take bus go home to your father. I get out, and a man, I never see him, he grab from behind and choking me. He choke and choke." She clenched her hands together and yanked them back and forth to simulate the assault. "I no can breathe, and I think I going to die. Then he stop." She sliced her hand through the air like a machete. "He tear the necklace from my neck, take my purse, so I turn to see him. You know what he do?" Disgust burrowed into her brow. "He punch me in the face because I look at him! He punch me and run. I try to chase, but he very fast. I yell and yell, but nobody come. That the way in Hong Kong, nobody helping."

I could picture her, pregnant and nearly strangled to death, picking herself up off the cement, and alone, in the middle of the night, giving chase to a vicious attacker. That was my mother.

The image was clear, but I could not feel for her. It brought to mind a story on the six o'clock news or a segment from *America's Most Wanted*, not the personal recounting of a traumatic incident happening to someone I cared about. And guilt flooded over me for what I didn't feel.

I stared at the bag on the ground. Why had she told me this? Why now?

* * *

The third hour of our flight and only eight more to endure. My lower back throbbed and my hip ached, but I didn't want to fight through an obstacle course of knees and trays to get up again. Normally, I liked to fly and enjoyed the takeoffs and landings the most. Maybe it stemmed from my initial trip to the US. Not old enough to understand the circumstances, I recalled the sensation of a carnival

ride. Now, as I watched a flight attendant help a doe-eyed
boy adjust his seat belt across the aisle, another memory
surfaced. Young, and without my mom, I wasn't scared. A
uniformed woman, perfumed with the scent of fresh-cut
flowers, kept bending down to check on me.

I turned to my mother. "Did I ever fly by myself when I
was a boy?"

She glanced at me out of the corner of her eye. "Hard to
remember."

But she came armed with an extraordinary memory.
My stepfather could attest to that. In their fights, she would
remind him in excruciating detail about a transgression
committed years before. Her recall, like a poisoned tip at the
head of a long spear, reached back to one's earliest mistakes.
I had been on the receiving end enough to know.

"A flight attendant kept reassuring me. She was very
friendly," I said.

"Let me think. Ah . . . I think so. I was hurry go
somewhere. For some reason, you not go, so I send for you."

What could possibly have been important enough to
abandon a child on an airplane?

An Asian flight attendant offered refreshments. My mom
asked for a soda, and I requested water. She sipped from her
cup, paused, and said, "Pretty face, that one. Eyes very round
and nose not flat, but mouth too big."

She relished picking out every flaw in a woman's
appearance, one of the reasons I never told her about
Quyen, a Vietnamese woman I met several months ago. We
were getting along; nothing to warrant back flips, except she
was the first Asian I ever dated—a major accomplishment
achieved through years of painstaking therapy—given
my lifelong aversion to anything Asian. Still, Quyen wasn't

Chinese, and I learned my lesson from Donna. Caucasian, separated, and even worse in my mother's unrelenting, razored scrutiny, Donna came with baggage—two children. So I didn't let on about Donna, but that didn't prevent my mom from finding out. The day I chose to take Donna and her kids for a dip in the pool at my parents' house, my mother happened to come home early from work, something she never did. So I introduced her to Donna and Jonathan and Timothy. Mom was pleasant and engaging, but while Donna changed the children in the bathroom, my mother pulled me into the kitchen and whispered, *"If you marry this one, I never speak to you again."* Then she turned and put glasses in the dishwasher as if she had just handed me the recipe for her fried wontons. I never forgave my mother for planting the seed which led to the eventual breakup of that relationship.

* * *

Seoul. I departed the plane with my head reeling and a twisted cord of quivering knots in my back. Mom's peppy gait suggested a willingness to launch into an extended search for the choicest flea markets in the vicinity.

We still needed to kill two hours before the connecting flight to Hong Kong. Worse, in the airport bathroom, I discovered a string of hives mottling my chin and neck.

In the waiting area, my mom peered out the wall of windows to the runway below and said, "We pretty close now."

"Yeah."

"Raymond, I want to say something."

I looked at her.

"If you see your father, you should give hug," she said.

"What?"

She hesitated and avoided eye contact. "Also should give some money, not lot, but is the custom for son your age."

I was dumbfounded. My mother telling me to embrace and give money to a man who hadn't so much as written me a note in nearly three decades!

After a long silence, I said, "I'm not going to do that."

"You should."

"Why?"

"That the Chinese way."

"I'm not Chinese."

She stared at a plane accelerating down the runway and remained silent as it lifted into the air.

Arrival 抵達

Chapter 2

My mother and I lugged our carry-ons through the maze of Hong Kong Kai Tak International Airport to the line for visitors entering the city. So many Chinese people everywhere: the same dungeon-black hair, thin bodies, and statures considered short by American standards. In the line for residents coming back to Hong Kong, a pair of loud voices broke through the din. I turned to see two men in tailored suits. One, holding an embossed leather briefcase, gestured emphatically. His companion didn't appear alarmed, so maybe that's how Chinese people talked.

Behind them with her family, a high school–aged girl wore a Calvin Klein T-shirt and Guess jeans. Auburn streaks tinted her straight, shoulder-length hair, and heavy blue eye shadow and garish red lipstick disguised her face. She would've fit right in at San Diego malls. I felt the strap of my travel bag biting into my shoulder, so I let it drop to my feet and wished it would transform into one of those rolling suitcases everyone else seemed to be wheeling. After my mom went through the passport checkpoint, I strolled up to the glass cubicle with my visa, where a stiff-postured man on a stool behind the partition spoke to me in Cantonese.

Taken by surprise, I shrugged. "Uh . . . I speak English."

He examined my passport, then me. "Arrival paper."

"Oh. Yes." I unzipped the travel pouch and handed him a slip.

He inspected it, regarded me again, and entered something into the computer. He studied the monitor and appeared to be gathering enough data to process an application for political asylum. Minutes passed. He punched in more information.

I shifted my feet, tugged on the strap of my pouch. My mom's visa came from the same country, so why didn't he ask for her arrival paper?

After hitting the keys for the third time and dissecting me with his gaze again, he stamped the tiny book and motioned me through.

I released my breath and walked toward my mother.

She said, "What take so long?"

"He asked me something in Chinese, and I answered in English. Maybe he didn't like my voice."

"Chee-se." Her attempt at saying "Jesus." She picked it up from my stepfather, who used it so much people must've thought he was in divinity school.

Bumping our way through a crush of elbows, shoulders, and luggage, we followed signs marked in both Chinese and English. Jammed with travelers, the airport, probably the size of San Diego's Lindbergh Field, seemed small.

Hong Kong was one of the world's busiest commercial centers, and lighted billboards and placards promoted everything from French perfume and Swiss watches to the latest pop singing sensation. Marketed toward the young, many boasted a Western flair. Couples in various stages of undress, in embraces seductive enough to earn an "R" rating, flaunted clothes with designer labels. American faces and bodies graced some of the ads, representing youth, vitality, and modern sex appeal. Funny, I couldn't recall displays in San Diego's airport depicting Asians.

At the baggage claim, I said to my mother, "Are you sure someone's going to meet us here?" When she didn't answer, I frowned.

After we retrieved the suitcases, I suggested we get a luggage cart.

"Prob-ly cost money," she said.

"We've just spent fifteen hours like caged hamsters. I don't know about you, but I'm not going to drag a bunch of suitcases around looking for people who might not even be here."

"If they not here, I call somebody else."

I grabbed a cart and brought it back. "It's free," I said, and stacked our bags on it.

We circled the waiting area twice with no sign of our welcoming party. Tired, sore, and jet-lagged, I could only think about unfurling on a soft pillow.

Mom continued to search with a worried expression. "Maybe they here. You wait. I go look some more. If no can find, I call my friend."

She started off, spun, and pointed at the baggage. "Make sure keep eye on. Very dangerous here."

Leaning against the cart, I checked my watch, rolled the loose leather band around my wrist, and waited, waited for my mother. My heart beat faster. A memory, my stepfather's agitated voice—the sour smell of alcohol and nicotine on his breath after a day out drinking—came back to me. *"Jesus Christ. Why does it always take your mother so long to get ready?"* He had planned for us to visit a friend—an old Navy beer buddy, now married with three stepdaughters—a family that didn't nag him about his drinking. I looked at my watch, an ill-fitting Timex with a dangling, brown plastic strap Roger had just given me for my tenth birthday. When my mom finally came out from the bedroom, Roger headed toward the door. She went straight into the kitchen to towel off some dishes. We never made it to the car that night. I hid in my room, clutching a pillow to my chest in the dark as the sounds of two people in the living room, intent on destroying each other, went on and on.

Now, I rolled my watchband around my wrist a few times. I bent over, straightened, tried to knead the tension out of my neck. Another fifteen minutes passed. I surveyed the throng of people, afraid my mom had gotten lost when she broke through the mass with three men.

She spoke to a balding, middle-aged man wearing glasses. Everything about him was round, from the domed forehead caused by his receding hairline, to the puffed crescents of his smiling cheeks, to his paunch belly.

The second guy, maybe in his thirties, trailed slightly behind. About my height, he presented a thicker frame and darker complexion.

The third man, in a short-sleeved, button-down print shirt and brown slacks, appeared older than the others. Like the first man, his hair had receded. He strode in unison with the younger fellow.

They drew closer, and the one by my mother stopped talking. All three men came to a halt and studied me as if I were the last of my species in the Galapagos. They moved nearer, and my mom put her hand on the shoulder of the man she had been talking to. "Raymond, this your uncle, Chun-Kwok."

I extended my hand and said, "Hi."

He smiled, welcoming me with a warm grasp.

I said to my mother, "They don't speak English?"

She shook her head and motioned toward the second

guy. "This Hoy. He your big cousin."

He gripped my hand and pumped it up and down twice. I said, "Good to meet you."

He broke into a wide grin. How strange to encounter full-grown "relatives" for the first time. The term never meant much to me. Mom always told me stories about an aunt or uncle or nephew in San Francisco or Houston or somewhere, but I could never relate. Sure, we shared some surface kinship, but how was I supposed to care about people I didn't know?

She pointed to the older man in the print shirt. "This your father."

I stared at him. Slim, like me, but shorter by four or five inches. The dark eyes, the narrow face and chin, the slight, flattened nose and thin upper lip, even the glistening sheen of his skin, were mine.

He reached for my hand and held it in a light, tentative manner, as if he didn't know how to touch me.

I realized I was staring and let go. He turned away.

The one introduced as my uncle took a suitcase from the cart. The cousin lifted another and my mother's travel bag while I held mine.

My father offered to carry my bag. "It's all right. I'll take it," I said.

He looked at me, then at the floor.

As we walked, I tried to take the suitcase from my uncle, who tightened his grip and said, "*Dak, dak, dak.*"

My mom said, "That mean he okay."

I followed them out of the airport into Hong Kong.

Hong Kong 香港

Chapter 3

The climate brought to mind with remarkable clarity how a lobster would feel in a vat of bubbling water. Hong Kong's suffocating humidity made it hard to breathe, and before long, my polo shirt and even my shorts stuck to me like moist tissue.

Thousands of narrow towers stretched skyward to prism the velvet night. The conglomeration of huddled structures made it difficult to tell where one building ended and the next began.

The air reeked of exhaust. Cars, taxis, and double-decker buses honked and hurtled in and out of the heap of confusion going down the wrong half of the street.

We jostled our way through the crowded sidewalks and came to an intersection, where Uncle Chun-Kwok took hold of my arm. The reason became apparent when cars zoomed by as if at Daytona. On these streets, vehicles clearly owned the right of way.

The signal changed, and we started across. I caught my father stealing peeks at me like a cheap private investigator.

Hard as I tried, I couldn't recall anything about my father. As a child, did I get along with him? Did we ever talk or was he like my stepfather, who spoke to me only when he wanted something? What was my mom's relationship with him? Did they fight? Is that why she left? And how could he willingly let her go with his son to another country, another world?

I fought the urge to look at him.

* * *

My uncle hailed two cabs. Before we entered, he communicated with my mom. My father came to me, placed his hand lightly on my shoulder, said something, pointed at himself and rotated his wrist, indicating somewhere else. He tapped my arm twice, turned, and disappeared into a taxi that sped off.

Without looking at me, my mother said, "He need to go work now. He working late, but he say he want to take us for dinner tomorrow."

We climbed into the waiting cab, Hoy in front, and my mom and I in back with Uncle Chun-Kwok. A steel mesh screen separated us from the driver, and I read the attached sign: "It is unlawful to smoke in the taxi."

My mother tested her hand on the metal barrier, and it held firm. "Wow, see how they need this?" She shook her head. "Very dangerous here."

* * *

My uncle lived in Aberdeen, a harbor town on the southern tip of Hong Kong. The cab let us off at what seemed to be an old office building in a business district with rows of closed shops facing us on both sides of the street. We entered a narrow, dingy lobby with putrid green paint peeling off the walls. It smelled of a musty gym and felt like a boiler room. At the elevator, Uncle Chun-Kwok greeted a shrunken, white-haired man hunched behind a rusted metal desk by the stairs. He must've been the guard because he stayed while we filed into the elevator.

We got out on the fourteenth floor and came up to a

sliding steel gate. My uncle unlocked it and spoke to my mom.

"He say they really lucky. He buy one house, and his wife have the one next door. They have two together; not many people have that."

He opened the barricade and we stepped into air-conditioning. A fan attached to the wall circulated cool air. A kitchen, the size of most bathrooms in America, stood across from a closet-like toilet near the front. Two rooms together at the end of the house, with a bunk bed taking up half the space in each, could fit inside my bedroom in San Diego.

A TV and a hexagonal aquarium sat on a counter protruding from the wall. The tank contained giant goldfish with bulbous eyes and vibrant colors. Above, a neatly lined row of books on a shelf. Higher, on a mantel, three ceramic figures, maybe a foot high, of long-bearded Chinese men—each with elaborate, ancient robes bestowing an air of importance. Still higher, enshrined on a wrought-iron stand, a framed black-and-white portrait of a man with even-cropped hair and studious eyes.

Beneath the counter, a large cardboard box of toys held board games and puzzles piled high. Folding trays and stools were stacked next to the box.

A woman in a light, short-sleeved beige sweater and dark blue shorts cuffed at the knees welcomed us with a smile. She wore a short, unadorned hairstyle reminiscent of a young Audrey Hepburn. My mother introduced her as Poi Yee, my aunt.

Aunt Poi Yee ushered us to a futon couch and waved for me to put down my travel bag. After we sat, she brought a folding tray and set out a large bowl of oval-shaped fruit protected by a rough skin the color of peanut shells.

My mom said, "*Dojeh*, Poi Yee." She reached into the bowl, separated one of the fruit from a waxy vine, and peeled the skin to reveal a berry resembling a skinless, green grape. "I don't know how to say this, but is good." She handed it to me. "Be careful the seed."

A unique taste, something between a grape and a kiwi, with a big pit in the middle.

From behind the door of a bedroom, two small heads, a girl's and a boy's, popped back and forth to spy on us. Seeing my aunt, they scrambled to their bunks, and she went into the room. My mother identified the ten-year-old girl as Jing-Wei and the seven-year-old boy as Ming, my uncle's children.

Hoy and Uncle Chun-Kwok took seats on stools near the TV and immersed themselves in conversation with my mom. Though most of their words sounded like gibberish, I recognized some phrases.

Laughter spilled out in loud voices, and sentences ended with last syllables carrying like the close of a song. Body gestures also accompanied the words; the upper torso of the speaker leaned forward with hands and arms thrusting and sweeping in constant motion. The fully animated face— eyes, mouth, brow, temples, and even the constricting and contracting neck muscles—added emphasis to an idea or opinion.

Laughter notwithstanding, an American watching might have thought they were arguing.

Soon, their gazes shifted to me, and I had the distinct feeling the discussion was about to veer in my direction. I plucked another piece of fruit from the bowl.

Hoy asked a question, and my mother shot a quick glance at me before responding. "He ask what you do, so I say you work for school, right?"

I nodded. The details of being a vocational counselor aspiring to become a marriage and family therapist would bring up more questions than I wanted to address. I dared not mention my interest in writing to avoid being seen as frivolous or worse.

Hoy, his face unable to contain his grin, said something to my mom. My uncle added a comment.

She said, "They ask if you have girlfriend."

My discomfort grew. How does one explain to relatives, upon first meeting, about a history of dysfunctional and destructive interpersonal relationships? Would they understand the term "codependency"? Somehow, going into my last two years of intense "inner child" work to deal with my unconscious self-sabotaging tendencies with women didn't seem quite the thing to do.

They trained their eyes on me, the complete and utter silence colluding in the eager anticipation of my response.

"I've been dating someone." I cupped the partially peeled piece of fruit in my hand and shook it like Vegas dice.

My mother told them, and Uncle Chun-Kwok said something to her.

"He say, is she Chinese?"

"Is that important?"

"'Course." Her tone reprimanded me for having to ask.

"She's Vietnamese. We're just getting to know each other."

The translation induced somber expressions, as if I'd announced the collapse of my business.

My uncle broke the silence, and they chuckled. My mother chimed along, and the three appeared to be having a royal time again.

She said, "They think you come to Hong Kong to find

Chinese wife."

My turn to wave my arms. "No, no. I'm just on vacation! Tell 'em, Mom. Tell 'em I'm just here on vacation."

Ignoring me, they started again, jabbering and snickering with my mother a ready accomplice.

"They say you should marry good Chinese girl so she teach you Chinese."

An avalanche of laughter, Hoy with his head back, blustering, Uncle Chun-Kwok holding his gut and slapping his leg in fits, my mom crowing, her whole body rocking.

I had been the butt of some good-natured teasing. Finally, the cackling subsided, and all I could do was shrug.

My mother shook a finger at me and said, "*Aiya, msik teng, msik gong.*" It meant, "Cannot understand, cannot speak," and the room erupted again.

Father 父親

Chapter 4

My mom and I waited with my uncle, aunt, and their children for a bus to take us to the Eastern District of Wan Chai. I felt nervous about meeting my father. I appreciated Uncle Chun-Kwok's hospitality but felt strange about the prospect of my father treating us to dinner. One question consumed my thoughts: why didn't he contact me?

My uncle, an off-duty bus driver, showed his company badge when the transport arrived, and we all rode for free. The moment the last person loaded on, the packed vehicle lurched forward, and I grabbed a handrail to keep from tumbling. We climbed the narrow steps to the upper level among passengers so squished together it reminded me of the contests to see how many bodies could be jammed into a VW. Did people ever get hurt? The mind-set must've been different from the US, where a woman could spill coffee in her own lap and win a lawsuit against McDonald's because no label warned of a hot beverage.

I sat by a window next to my mother and observed the activity in the streets below. Vendors in threadbare jeans hawked newspapers and magazines on street corners, and merchants set out produce and dried meats on makeshift tables at tiny stalls piled with empty wicker baskets and cardboard boxes. These crude stands competed close to modern multistoried department stores which would've looked right at home in La Jolla. Older folks in simple, dark-toned peasant clothing walked alongside men in executive suits. A constant rush of people crammed the sidewalks, their voices lost in the trumpet of blasting car horns on the congested roads.

I asked my mom, "How long have you known Uncle Chun-Kwok and Aunt Poi Yee?"

"Many years. I know him first. He very nice, always treat me good," she said.

"You met him through my father?"

She paused. "Your uncle run away from China, stay at my house in Hong Kong."

"He lived with you and my father?"

"He write from China, say he want to come to Hong Kong. After I take you to America, he keeping in touch with me. When he run to Hong Kong, I let him stay my house."

"Your house?"

"I work hard, you know that. Your father not work a lot, so I not know if we can ever buy house. House good, should have for family, so I borrow money from my sister to buy."

"How did my father feel about that?"

"He not say, but house good, I tell you that," she said. "I living with your father in the house little bit. Your father move out the house after we go, so when his brother come to Hong Kong, I let him stay my house."

The bus pulled to a screeching stop, and our group exited to a crush of pedestrians. I was usually protective about my personal space. Here, with four individuals to every square foot of land, breathing room was a luxury I couldn't afford.

Uncle Chun-Kwok spoke, and Mom translated, "We have to be very careful. He say many people steal in Hong Kong."

"Why is that?"

"Many people run away from Canton, but no can find job. No choice, have to eat."

My mother said it as if she understood all too well. I knew little of her past before we came to the US. She was born in China and met my father there. When the Communists came to power, the two fled separately to Hong Kong. They married, but she never said why they divorced.

"How was it for you here?" I asked.

"Life always hard in Hong Kong."

"Is that why you left?"

She hesitated, then spoke with a harsh edge in her voice. "We do good business, have house. Michael go to school. Renee go to school. You have good education, job. What you think?"

* * *

We waded through the crowd to a men's clothing store, and my uncle took us in. Looking fashionable in a sea-green polo, dark blue slacks, and seal-brown oxfords, he inspected some shirts, then went to a rack of warm-up suits. He fingered a gray fleece set with pants and hooded top and spoke to my mom.

"He want to buy for you," my mother said. "He say good quality, so you try on."

"Tell him he doesn't have to do that."

"I think he want to."

"Just tell him."

She paused before relaying it.

He took another suit from the rack.

"He want to buy for you."

Receiving gifts always made me uncomfortable. When I was a child, my stepfather asked what I wanted for

Christmas. I couldn't answer, so he turned to my mother and said, *"Fine. He's your son. You get him something."* Other kids hosted birthday parties and invited friends, but I never wanted a celebration and even asked my teacher not to have one for me at school. On my birthday, I often skipped class altogether.

Giving was different; it meant more. In the fifth grade I saved my lunch money to buy my mom a present for her birthday. I remember going to the K-Mart jewelry counter with my $8.50 in quarters to ask the sales lady for help. I probably spent an hour looking at the various bracelets, necklaces, and earrings before choosing a pirate's treasure chest jewelry box because I liked the feel of the royal, red-felt interior.

I watched Uncle Chun-Kwok run his hand along the inner lining of a crimson, nylon warm-up jacket. I said to my mom, "Tell him he's really kind, but I have lots of clothes."

My uncle persisted. Despite my protests, he went to a display of designer leather belts inside a glass counter and spoke.

She said, "Wow! Very expensive. He want to buy."

I walked up to him, put my hands on his shoulders, and peered through his glasses into his eyes. "Please, I really don't need anything. If you want to buy something, get it for your family." I motioned at Jing-Wei and Ming, both watching with rapt attention.

Uncle Chun-Kwok looked at me; the disappointment on his face sent a wave of guilt through me. He nodded once, turned, and headed toward the exit. As we followed him, a part of me wanted to express my regret, but I didn't.

Outside on the crowded street, I watched my uncle and Ming. They walked together, my cousin's small hand

wrapped in his father's. Earlier, we had taken a ferry to
dine at the Jumbo Floating Restaurant, an imperial seafood
palace that seemed to literally float on the water. Uncle
Chun-Kwok kept putting more food in his son's bowl, and
Ming kept eating. I tapped my mother's shoulder and asked
her to tell my uncle it was amazing that Ming possessed such
a healthy appetite.

Uncle Chun-Kwok smiled and talked in a manner that
conveyed a profound regard for his children.

"He say Ming eat good, will grow big and strong.
Jing-Wei more picky, but she going to be very smart. He
say lucky for them to have boy and girl, good balance." She
paused and added, "I remember they marry and want to
have kids, but no have luck first few years. They so happy
when they have Jing-Wei."

Aunt Poi Yee, who had gone ahead with her daughter,
called to us, and my uncle strode faster to catch up.

My mom said, "If Uncle Chun-Kwok stay in China, can
only have one kid, so good for him come here."

"I can't imagine China being more crowded than this."

"But here nobody tell you how many kids can have."

After a silence, I said, "Is that why a lot of Chinese
people escape into Hong Kong?"

She nodded.

"How are they able to do that?"

"Sometimes, they come visit, not go back."

"They don't check documents here?"

"'Course. Police ask for I.D. card. You not have, they take
you back."

"So what did my uncle do?" I asked, knowing the answer
would divulge much about how she fled China.

"He hide. Need place to live, so good he know me."

I glanced ahead to keep track of our group. "So Uncle Chun-Kwok used your house."

"Yes. He find work and get Hong Kong I.D."

"People will hire you?"

"You work hard, they give job."

Not so different from San Diego, where a major political issue involved undocumented Mexicans crossing the border. The bigwigs poured funds into beefing up the Border Patrol and building fences, but as long as employers were willing to hire, there would be no shortage of undocumented labor. The issue proved delicate, however, when it came to light that some of the most vocal proponents of anti-immigration legislation had employed cheap, undocumented workers themselves.

Both my parents and my uncle had escaped from China. It made me want to see what they were running from.

"We're going to China, right?" I asked.

"If enough money, we go. See how much we spend here first."

"We're so close. We should—"

At the entrance of a restaurant, Uncle Chun-Kwok gestured toward the double glass doors. He pushed through to hold one side open for us. My aunt and her children waited in the lobby.

I stepped in and felt my heart hammering at the thought of my father being there. I drew a deep breath, saw Ming, and felt a sudden urge to rub my hand against his stubby hair.

I did so, and he spun and stared at me as if I had just snatched the chocolate lava cake from his dessert bowl.

His short hair showed his widely protruding ears and the bulb shape of his head. He didn't look too different from pictures of me at his age, although the neon strobes flashing in the clear, cushiony heels of his tennis shoes weren't around then.

I mussed his hair again, and this time, he poked me in the stomach.

I turned to Aunt Poi Yee, who smiled. I watched my uncle, walking with his hand on Jing-Wei's shoulder. Ming kept craning his head back to keep his eye on me as we climbed the stairs to the restaurant above.

* * *

At the top of the stairs, the maitre d' led us through a spacious and formal dining area. Long, vertical plate-glass windows looked out on the bustle of pedestrians and vehicles in the streets below. Groups of patrons engaged in loud, animated discussions at round tables draped in white linen, and no empty stations could be seen.

We passed two huge water tanks, one with an array of live fish, the other crawling in shellfish. Ming stopped to gawk at the underwater creatures, and my uncle nudged him to keep going.

I became conscious of the other diners—men with silk ties and designer wool suits and women in sequin-beaded dresses and flashy high heels—while I wore a T-shirt and jeans. Why, after all these years, did my father bring me to such a fancy restaurant? Had he been in touch with my mom? Did he even know anything about me?

My father was a forbidden subject, like adultery or alcoholism. My mother never mentioned him, as if he didn't exist, and I never asked.

I fixed on the flashing red lights in the heels of Ming's shoes and followed them. The host directed us to the middle of the restaurant where a gathering awaited us at a gigantic table. I saw my father, his wispy, thinning black hair, the restaurant's fluorescent light casting a glow off his forehead's dove-white skin, his dark eyes half-hidden, almost shuttered by the narrow slats of his eyelids. He wore a pale, oversized button-down print shirt that hung loose on his hunched, spiny shoulders. He got up to greet us, and at full height, he stood a shade over five feet. Still, he was taller than my mom. He pulled out the chair next to him, and the host guided me there.

My mother sat on my right. To my father's left, a woman with short, straight hair bounced a baby in a fuzzy yellow sleeper on her lap. A toddler occupied a booster seat alongside her. I recognized my cousin Hoy, sporting a white muscle T-shirt and a carefree grin. The man adjacent to Hoy resembled my uncle, but was thinner, with a narrow, jutting jaw and a chipmunk-shaped mouth. Sunken pockets under his eyes made him look tired. Next came a chubby teenage boy with wide bulging eyes, magnified by thick glasses, giving his face the impression of shock or dismay. He sat with another boy, a little younger and thinner. A girl with straight hair parted off center, about the same age as Jing-Wei, remained expressionless by the two boys. And finally, a woman, with flabby cheeks and a mole on her chin, smiled at us. Uncle Chun-Kwok and his family settled into the empty seats near this woman.

I whispered to my mom, "Who are all these people?"

"Maybe that his family." She stared at the woman holding the infant.

"His wife?"

"Could be."

"I have a stepmother?"

She shrugged.

My father introduced my mom and me to the others at our table. She greeted each one, and I nodded, smiled, and waved.

Then she said, "The woman with the little girl and baby, she Hoy's wife."

Relief swept over me. Hard enough to meet a father I didn't know. Thank God I didn't have to deal with a stepmother too.

"The one by Hoy, he Huang Fu. He also your uncle, youngest brother to your father. He one of seven sons in family."

"Seven?"

"Yes. Your father have two older brothers, number one, number two in China. Your father number three. Number four in China too. Number five die last year. Chun-Kwok, we stay with him, he number six. Huang Fu number seven."

It felt like the first day at work, when they introduced you to the one hundred and thirty-six people in your department.

She pointed to Hoy. "He the son to Number One."

I nodded.

"The girl and two boys belong to Number Seven. The woman with, how you say, spot, moling on face? She the one his wife."

"Got it." My circuits had long since overloaded. At least I didn't have to speak.

My father offered a bottle of Hennessy. I shook my head.

He solicited the others. The takers were Hoy and Number Seven. I sipped my orange juice.

My father poured tea, and my mom tapped three fingers in front of her cup to show thanks, so I followed her lead.

She said, "Your father have two sisters, one in Hong Kong, but she not here."

I asked her why.

"They not invite. For Chinese people, men more important than women."

She said it as if stating a well-known fact. Strange that my mother, a woman whose very presence commanded the authority of an army drill sergeant, would come from a culture that viewed her as unimportant. I felt a tap on my shoulder and turned to see my father holding a glossy jewelry store shopping bag. He placed it on my lap and motioned for me to peek inside.

My mom said, "I think he give you, so you say, '*Dojeh*' when he done."

Not again. What was it about this city and gifts? I said, "I can't take his presents."

"He give you in front of family. Look bad if you not accept."

I scanned the table, all eyes on me. Amidst the clattering of dishes and the buzz of intermingled background conversations, I felt all alone. With reluctance, I reached into the bag and brought out a black leather billfold with an Italian label stamped in silver. I looked at my father, "Thank you, uh . . . *Dojeh*."

He pointed to the bag.

More? What about the others? Don't they get some? I took out a cloth pouch with the word "madler" on it. The contents smelled of new leather. I untied the pouch to reveal a black handbag with an embedded brass "m."

I extended it to my mother. "It's a purse. Maybe this is for you."

A sad smile. "Not for me. You the son. He buy for you. In

Hong Kong, many men carry this."

My arms felt icy and numb. The air-conditioning, such
a relief when we entered, now chilled me to my core. I said,
"*Dojeh*," to my father in a quiet voice.

He touched the bag, indicating more. All eyes around the
table were still riveted on me.

After never sending me so much as a letter, why did
this man bother with gifts? The next item was a little white
box with "LONGINES" in emerald-green logotype. Inside,
propped against a small satin pillow rested a luxurious gold
quartz watch with a silver and gold chain-mesh band.

I shook my head. "I can't accept all this."

He pointed to the bag again.

I looked at my mom. She didn't say anything. I turned
back to him. "I really can't—"

He put his hand on mine and said, "Man-Kit" while
gesturing to the bag once more. I didn't move, so he reached
in and removed an elegant rectangular box the color of red
wine edged in a gold border. "S.J. Dupont, PARIS" shone in
glittering letters. My father placed the box in my palm.

As I stared at it, he tapped the flat surface, and I opened
the box. A matching case with the same words in gold. I
lifted the lid to unveil the most exquisite writing instrument
I had ever seen. It sparkled like jewelry—thin, with a
smooth, shiny surface black as onyx. The tip, the middle, and
the pocket clip gleamed in shimmering gold.

I picked it up and rotated it. It felt perfect in my hand.
I read the words engraved in the gold center of the pen:
"LAQUE DE CHINE, S.J. Dupont, PARIS."

I whirled in my seat to my mother. "He knows I write?"

"Maybe Uncle tell him." Her voice a bare whisper.

I held the gift. In a few moments, I asked her what my

father said to me moments ago.

"Man-Kit, that your Chinese name, Wong Man-Kit."

My Chinese name. So long ago. Man-Kit . . . "*Mon-key, mon-key, mon-key* . . ." That's how the kids taunted me the first days of school in America. I didn't react, didn't give them the satisfaction. I refused to tell or run crying home. I curled my fingers into fists. They didn't stop.

Gripping the pen, I peered into my father's eyes and said, "*Dojeh.*"

He clasped my hand and gave it a light squeeze.

This man, whom I hadn't seen for so many years, who I thought didn't care about me, just presented me the best gift I had ever received.

I studied my father. For the first time, I felt I meant something to him.

Request 要求

Chapter 5

My father ordered the food, and the presentation of each dish elicited a cascade of
"Oohs" and "Ahhs" from our group. The waiter brought what appeared to be the carved outer half of a watermelon. He ladled brothy soup from the interior; my mom referred to it as *don qua jon*. It contained scallops and shrimp blended with thick slices of soft white melon.

Next came rice and a course of seasoned jumbo shrimp in whole shells. Then an entire steamed freshwater fish bathed in a flavorful, salty sauce. The vegetables included a heaping serving bowl of stir-fried red spinach and another with Chinese broccoli—my uncle called it *gai-lan*—in a tangy oyster sauce. A plate of steamed squash stuffed with scallops followed. After this, a mound of baked mud-crab filled the air with the aroma of garlic and ginger.

The waiter put an oval tray on the serving wheel at our table, and we rotated it for everyone to sample. As each plate circled, my father retrieved a portion for me, which I appreciated. My proficiency with chopsticks ranked right up there with my fluency in Cantonese.

Boisterous conversation flowed at our table. I recognized some phrases and a pattern to the communication. The men were louder and spoke more. The one my mother referred to as Number Seven, my father's youngest brother, talked so fast that I couldn't begin to understand, his rapid clip presenting a sharp contrast to the fatigue on his face heightened by the deep bags under his eyes.

A friendly one-upsmanship developed between Number Seven and my cousin Hoy. The cousin's stories induced hearty laughter from listeners, but Number Seven's bids for attention with emphatic arm and hand gestures, wide, exaggerated facial expressions, and even his forward-leaning torso added drama to his tales. He also spoke at every turn, but the combination of a devilish glint in my cousin's eyes and his "little innocent me" grin pushed everyone to the brink of hysterics. They were born showmen, and my father and Uncle Chun-Kwok could only sit and watch these two performers in action.

The women nodded and laughed. My aunt stayed silent for the most part, and Hoy's wife appeared too busy with her baby and toddler to join the revelry. Number Seven's wife, perhaps trying to keep up with her husband's breakneck pace, provided follow-up to his monologues.

Number Seven's oldest son asked him many questions, but his other children didn't speak. I observed the talkative teenage boy's protruding eyes and fought to suppress a chuckle—he seemed to be in a state of shock at his father's sustained gabbiness. Mom remained surprisingly reserved. Always the center of attention, she could cast her own spell upon a rapturous audience. Now, she just listened.

I said, "You're quiet tonight."

She gazed at the rice and stuffed squash in her bowl. "Nothing to say. Not know many people here."

But she was at her best in those situations. I always marveled at the way she warmed new customers at her restaurant with insightful and disarming comments about their work or families. In the space of minutes, she developed enough rapport to needle them with gentle humor.

Number Seven's wife questioned my mother, who said to me, "She ask what you do."

I hesitated. My role as a career counselor seemed safer than revealing my desire to eventually own a private practice treating people with marital issues. I read that Chinese people dealt with problems by keeping them in the family. They sought advice from elders and, in rare cases, trusted friends. Never would one bear the shame of consulting a stranger about personal matters.

I jabbed at a piece of fish in my bowl. "Tell her I help people."

Number Seven reached for some mud-crab and spoke to my mom.

"He say, what people?"

"People who have lost their jobs; some of them are trying to change careers." Best to leave out the family therapy part and the corresponding images of Jack Nicholson and his *Cuckoo's Nest.*

Number Seven spoke again, and my mother relayed. "He say why they need you? Why they not just go look for work?"

"Some people don't know what they want, and others need more skills."

Another discussion.

"They say, you tell people what job is good?"

This was getting more complicated. I drank some orange juice. Bitter. "Not exactly."

A circle of puzzled expressions. Before I could explain further, Aunt Poi Yee broke in, and soon, comprehension registered on their faces.

I scooted closer to my mom. "What did she say?"

My mother pried the shell from a jumbo shrimp. "She say some people want find new job, but they scared. You help them try something new, but not easy do that."

I gave an appreciative nod to my aunt, who smiled.

I turned to my mother and said, "What does my father do?"

"How I know?"

"Do you know anything about him?"

She didn't reply.

"Can you ask?"

My mom hesitated, but did so. My father regarded me, refilled his glass of cognac, and responded.

She said, "He work at nightclub, do bookkeeping."

"Does he like it?"

Another exchange. "He say it make money."

"Where does he live?"

He took a drink, then answered. Again, she paused. "He live close by. He say can show us later."

"All right."

She told him, and he smiled at me.

"What about Hoy and his wife? What do they do?"

My mother spun the serving wheel and stopped it with the fish tray in front of her. She used chopsticks to bring some fish to her bowl. "I know he work, build houses. She take care the baby and little girl."

"And Number Seven?"

A long response from him. She said, "He own restaurant, is outside, but he making good money."

"Outside? An outdoor café?"

"I think so."

"His wife works there too?"

"They have three kids, so she stay home."

Of the four women at our table, three were housewives. Maybe that was the Chinese way. How did my mom, twenty-eight years ago, care for me, maintain the home, support my father, and still have the foresight to buy a house in this culture?

Number Seven said something, and I prepared for another of his stories. Instead, he patted his oldest son's head and took out papers to show everyone.

My mother put down her chopsticks, received the papers, thumbed through them, and made comments. She passed them to my father, who shuffled them to Hoy's wife.

"They report cards. He say the son do very good in school, but to me, he not look so smart."

It must've been important for Chinese people to brag about their children. Uncle Chun-Kwok swelled with pride when he talked about Jing-Wei and Ming, and now, Number Seven was handing out transcripts. Funny, but my mother never did that with me. In fact, she went to the other extreme in comparing me to her friend's son, Jason. Chinese, my age, and perfect in every way, he helped his parents, boasted stellar grades, and spoke flawless Cantonese. I hated him. Whenever I messed up, my mother would break into a chorus of *"Jason not talk back to parents."* Or *"They never have to tell Jason take out trash."* Or *"Jason never get 'C' in school."*

I pleaded with God to inflict Jason with just one flaw, a wart on his eyelid, a fear of potato bugs, sweaty armpits, anything. I resented not only Jason but also the expectation to achieve. Graduating high school with honors wasn't enough. My mother demanded I go to college, earn a degree, and vault into a prestigious, high-paying career. I chose social services. I wanted to do something meaningful, but at least part of the reason I entered such a low-paying and little-recognized field came in direct response to the intense pressure to succeed.

I turned my attention to Number Seven's other children. I said to my mom, "What about the other boy and the girl? Are their grades good, too?"

"He not have report cards for them. Maybe he like the older one more."

The grade slips circulated. Number Seven studied me and made a remark while pointing to his jaw.

"He say he know how to make rash better. He have tea at home for you."

Great, now everyone was staring at my complexion. On the flight from L.A. to Seoul, my chin and neck had broken out like a bad case of mumps. "Tea?"

"That what he say."

"How's tea going to help my skin?"

"He say have to clean inside the body first. Tea good for that. If not do, it come back."

Nodding and cajoling, he waved at me with his chopsticks. While I contemplated, my father, swirling a glass of cognac in hand, spoke to my mother.

At first, she listened, but as he continued, she shrank into her seat, motionless.

A pall descended on our group. Even Number Seven grew quiet. Around us, things appeared normal. People chatted and ate, waiters served, busboys rattled dishes, diners followed the maitre d' to empty seats, and patrons got up to leave. But at our table, everything stopped. It reminded me of *The Twilight Zone*.

All attention shifted to my mom and her sudden, eerie silence.

I had never seen her like this. Stubborn, calculating, and spiteful, yes, but always in control. I didn't know what to make of this shell-shocked form next to me.

In time, the focus returned to her eyes. She looked at me with a vacant vestige of her usual demeanor and said in a quiet voice, "He ask you go to China. He want you meet his brothers and family. He want you go see . . . the place how you say for people die?"

"Cemetery? Grave?"

She nodded. "He want you go see grave of his parents."

A few days ago, I didn't know this man. Now he was inviting me to accompany him to China to meet more of his family and see his parents' graves. My mother's reaction and the silence at our table spoke to the importance of his request. "How do you feel about this?"

It took her a moment to answer. "Okay. No problem for me."

"You want to go?"

"He ask you."

"I can't even talk to him."

My mom remained quiet.

I peered at her. "Maybe this isn't such a good idea."

She regarded me, then stood and walked across the restaurant toward the restrooms. I started to get up, but saw Aunt Poi Yee already headed in that direction.

Many minutes later, they returned. Without looking at anyone, my mother sat in her seat. She said, "Okay. No problem. You go, I go. We go together."

"I don't understand."

"No have to worry. We go."

I studied her. "You're sure?"

She nodded.

I paused before saying, "Okay."

Number Seven announced it, and the people at our table came back to life, except for Mom, who stayed solemn and still, staring into her cup of cold tea.

I picked up the teapot and poured some into her cup. She didn't tap the table. Her eyes seemed distant and lost, and her shoulders slumped, like the stem of a plant, once strong and vibrant, now wilting and slowly dying inside.

Dwelling 安頓

Chapter 6

At the end of the meal, the waiter brought a platter of fresh watermelon slices, cantaloupe spears, and orange segments for dessert. He signaled to my father, who motioned his hand in the manner of a king being served at his throne. Next came hot towels. And the check.

My father snatched it from the table. Uncle Chun-Kwok, Hoy, and Number Seven called out, all gesturing toward the ticket. My father shook his head, and a battle ensued. The three of them tried to wrest the bill from him, but he pressed it to his chest like a precious photograph and brushed people away.

When they relented, he put a wad of cash on the ticket tray. The waiter brought change. As my father got up to leave, he put some Hong Kong hundred-dollar notes on the table.

Our entire party walked together through the restaurant and down the stairs to an expansive lobby with mirrored walls and towering pillars painted in ornate, floral patterns. The group gathered to bid each other good night. Then, my father led Uncle Chun-Kwok and his family, my mother, and me into the muggy night.

A swarm of shoving pedestrians greeted us on the sidewalks of Wan Chai. Above rows of crowded shops, neon signs promoted businesses in Chinese characters. Many included English in smaller letters. Three- and four-story tenements, with rickety balconies, butted up against the

still-open shops and restaurants. Lines of clothing hung
from many of the dwellings; it struck me as an act of futility
in this moist air.

A few blocks later, we turned into the narrow entrance of
a lobby grungier than Uncle Chun-Kwok's. The eroded paint
left cracked patches of mud-colored undercoatings, and in
some sections, huge holes in the plaster appeared to have
gone untended for years. It smelled like a moldy attic.

Nobody guarded this lobby. We loaded into a cramped,
creaky elevator. While my father and uncle conversed, I held
my breath as the lift cables squealed to protest our combined
weight. The elevator ascended in hitched agony before
picking up speed. It jolted to a stop at the eleventh floor, and
I let out a muffled "Phew" when the door opened.

My father guided us through a tiny corridor to a
heavy iron-railed screen. He unlocked it and slid it open
to herd us into a tight entry hall where a dormlike facility
presented a kitchen and doors farther down on both sides.
A stooped, bare-chested, middle-aged man with a wrinkled
belly emerged from one of the rooms. My father greeted
him in a casual tone and introduced me, then my mom, who
had slipped into silence again. The man mumbled a reply
without acknowledging us, shuffled to the refrigerator, took
out a beer bottle, and headed back to his room.

My father spoke to me and pointed to the refrigerator.
My mother said, "He ask if you want something to drink."

A communal refrigerator?

I shook my head. My father went to a cabinet above the
sink and took out a tumbler. He brought down one of the
three bottles of Hennessy from the top of the refrigerator,
and as he poured, my mom shook her head and said, "He
drink a lot."

My father offered the cognac to my mother, who reacted as if he had extended a cup of battery acid. He asked Uncle Chun-Kwok and Aunt Poi Yee, but both declined.

My father took a swallow and looked at us standing in his kitchen. He set the glass on the counter, hurried down the hall, opened a cupboard, and lifted out some short stools. It took two trips to carry back enough stools for all of us. He swept dust off the wooden surfaces with his hand before directing us to sit.

I sat by the refrigerator in a kitchen a bit larger than my uncle's, with just enough space to hold seven people. A gray, rectangular sink, the kind found in American garages, was piled full of dishes next to a rusty stove with two burners.

I leaned toward my mom and said, "Does he own this place?"

She asked my father, who shook his head. He got up, said something, and motioned for me to follow him down the hallway. We went into a room where a single bed, little more than an army cot, took up most of the area. At the foot of it, a chest of drawers supported a small TV. I saw loose change and an assortment of toiletry items scattered on the dresser and a pile of unlaundered shirts and pants strewn on the floor. A small window opposite the door provided a brick-wall view of the adjacent building.

Hard to imagine anyone living in these confines. If my father resided here, how could he afford such an expensive dinner and all the gifts? A wave of sadness washed over me. I had been with my stepfather long enough to see how isolated a man could be even in a house full of people. Now, I could picture my father here by himself. After work, he would walk back to this dilapidated building, take that shaky elevator up, unlock the barricade, and reach for a bottle at the top of the refrigerator. He would get a glass from the cabinet, pour himself some cognac, and bring it to this room. Then he would undo his tie, toss it on the pile of clothes, switch on the TV, and settle into the cot with only his drink for company.

I looked at my father and forced a smile.

I thanked him for showing me his room.

* * *

Afterwards, my father talked to Uncle Chun-Kwok, and my mother chatted with Aunt Poi Yee. Soon, Ming hopped over and launched himself with his chest atop my father's knee. Sitting on a stool, the man wrapped his arm around his nephew and tugged on the boy's mousy ears while my cousin shrieked in delight. Ming managed to work free from the hold and scooted behind his uncle to pull on his ears from behind. My father laughed and hung his head in a mock expression of pain.

Watching them made me smile. As he clowned with Ming, my father appeared lighthearted, and my cousin seemed to relish the attention. Did my father ever do that with me? Did he ever encircle me in his long, wiry arms and lift me into the air, twirling me above his head the way he was spinning my cousin now? And did I holler out in unfettered bliss?

How much time did my father spend with Ming? Did Uncle Chun-Kwok bring his family to visit often? I hoped so, because I preferred this picture of my father, engaged in frivolous play with a member of his family, to the image of him, somber and alone, in his room.

Survival 生存

Chapter 7

Late in the evening at my uncle's house I lay on the futon in the living room listening to the steady drone of the air conditioner. I thought about the dinner and my mother's unusual demeanor. Did it make her uncomfortable to see my father? Could it have been the gifts? Her voice sounded so subdued when I asked if he knew about my writing. And the meal. How hard must it have been for her to watch her former husband order dish after dish of the finest foods for us, to see him fending off his family's attempts to share the cost? Mom always scrimped. She would clip coupons, wait 'til the last day to pay bills, and buy at garage sales. My father probably spent more on our dinner than she had in eating out the whole year. The lavish feast made me uncomfortable, yet my father had invited his family to meet me, and he selected a gift that meant so much. Did he ask about me? Is that how he knew about my writing? Was he trying to make up for lost time? Or was it guilt at—

A light flickered on in my mother's room. The door squeaked open and she slipped through the living room to the kitchen. I heard the sound of the refrigerator opening, followed by the "fwip" of it shutting, the clinking of ice cubes, and the splash of liquid being poured.

As she made her way back I whispered, "Mom?"

She stopped and said in a hushed voice, "How come you not go sleep?"

"I was thinking."

She came to me with a glass of ice water in her hand. "I not sleeping good, too."

"What'd you think about the dinner?"

In the faint light from her room I watched her walk toward the T.V. With glass still in hand she pulled out a stool from under the counter, carried it over, and sat beside me. She took a drink, then said, "Your father spend lots money. He should not do that."

"Maybe he thought it was a special occasion."

"Wow, the fish, you know that cost more than eight hundred dollars Hong Kong." Her frown deepened the lines on her forehead. "That one hundred dollars American, for fish! He crazy."

A tense silence hung between us.

I looked across the room at the three ceramic figures partially cloaked in shadow on the shelf. One of them, bald and with a long white beard, stood hunched. Another wore an elaborate, ancient robe with matching formal headpiece. The third, in similar garb, though not as decorative, grasped a thick cane. "What do those three statues represent?"

She tracked my gaze. "They very old. Many Chinese people have that in house. One mean for long life. One mean good luck for money. One mean happiness for family."

"What about the picture above?" The large framed portrait of a grim-faced man stared back at me in the dim light.

"Prob-ly he the father to your uncle or the father to Poi Yee."

Stationed high and centered on the wall, he surveyed the entire house. It felt eerie having him observe us.

"Was it hard for you tonight?"

She turned back to me and said, "What you mean?"

"Being there with my father, eating with his family."

My mother paused. "Not so bad. They very nice. But Number Seven, he talking too much about the older son. You see how he show the grades for him? Really, the boy not look so smart." She shook her head.

"Maybe he was proud of him."

"What about the daughter? She just sit there. Even the middle boy, Number Seven talk to him little bit, but he never talk to the girl."

I could see the daughter in my mind, blank-faced, so still, ignored. I knew how she felt because that's how my stepfather treated me. It didn't upset me, but Roger was different with my brother. When Michael was born, Roger went to the hospital every day until my mother came home with their baby. The man pampered her those first months. He stopped going to bars after work and helped with the laundry and shopping. He began staying out again, but still dropped off toys and clothes for Michael. As my brother grew, Roger drove him to school, attended his high school football games, and even financed his education at USC. My stepfather didn't do these things for me, but I could never resent my brother. We always had a good relationship, and I would help my mom take care of him and my sister, Renee.

One thing did bother me. Roger said I was his son, yet he never adopted me. Maybe in his mind, he didn't need to since we lived under the same roof, but it felt strange to know the name I used at school wasn't the one on our mailbox.

I peered at my mother. "You think he loves his older son more than his other children?"

"That how he do."

"You feel bad for the girl?"

"He should not treat her like that. Maybe she do good in school too, but she not have chance."

Her eyes held a faraway look, one of deep reflection. I said, "Can you tell me about your life in Hong Kong?"

She stared into the glass in her hand, took a drink. "Very hard. Many people, and very dangerous."

"That's what you said earlier."

"You not believe? You ask Uncle. He tell you."

"No, it's not that. I was just remembering what you said about the man who attacked you."

"That true. You see how dangerous in Hong Kong before? That the way now, too."

"Is that why you left?"

She sat unmoving, clenching the glass. In time she said, "I born in Canton, you know."

I nodded.

"My hometown called Tai Shan, very small. Many people poor. But my father not poor. He have good education. In China before, they give test to see who smart. My father do very good, so the government give him land, and he rent for people grow rice."

"That was enough to support your family?"

"Sure. We very happy. But in 1949, the Communists come. They take over my hometown. They jealous my father because he have land, so take him to jail."

She put the glass to her mouth, swallowed the last of the liquid. She looked at the ice melting in the glass. "They take him and . . ." Her hands shook; her voice grew quiet. "And . . . they shoot him."

She sat, head down, eyes staring into a void. "They not have to do that. He not hurt them."

I didn't know what to say. For the first time, my mom looked old to me. Deep lines marked her forehead and the tiny, tired edges of her eyes. Small age spots marred her cheeks and neck, and streams of white coursed through her nest of black hair.

"They put my mother in jail, never let her go."

"I'm sorry, Mom."

"They have guns, so nobody stop them." She said it in an even, flat tone. "My mother tell me run away. No can stay when they do that."

"How old were you when this happened?"

"Twelve."

"Only twelve?"

"Have to go, no choice."

"How did you live?"

"Cook and clean for people. I go to stay with cousin. We taking care of rabbits and chickens. She very poor, but I ask for money. I not want do that, but no choice."

A twelve-year-old fleeing alone through China, cooking and cleaning for bowls of rice to eat—what must that have been like? "How long did you live with your cousin?"

"She help me stay her house two years. But I feel bad she take care for me, because she so poor, so I go. I find own place, different town. The place I live for poor people. The front wall broke down, two level, but very old. Climb ladder to go up. No curtain for window, have to hang towel. No bathroom. Walk long way for water."

"You lived there on your own?"

"Yes, I stay in China until nineteen. Take care by myself. Hard for live in China, so I try go to Hong Kong. I need write fake letters from my mother, say she sick in Hong Kong so the people in China can let me go visit her. When they let me go visit, I stay."

"You knew my father in China, then met again in Hong Kong?"

"Yes, he run from China, I not know when, but prob-ly before I go. In Hong Kong, the Kowloon side, we see each other on street. He want to talk. I not know a lot people, so I say okay. I tell him place I stay. He come to talk a lot. I think must be he have good job let him do that. If I not there, he just come the next day."

"What did you think of him?"

"I nineteen, what I know? He talk very nice, say he want take care for me. My life very hard by myself. I think maybe I can have house, family again." She looked down at the red and gold flower embroidered at the top of her black cloth slipper.

"Were you happy together?"

"At first, okay. He work some, do bookkeeping. I work at a sewing machine factory, sew the men's shirts. But he lose job after I have you. I scared we not have enough money."

"Did you tell him about this?"

"No. He not the kind person can talk like that." Her tone made me feel silly for asking.

I pushed myself up on the futon, remembering all the times she had chastised me to sit straight when I was a child. "Is that why you left Hong Kong?"

"Your father not working much. I have older sister in China." She paused and gave me a contemplative look. "She come to Hong Kong, too. She the one I borrow money to buy house for family. But after that man choking me, I know Hong Kong too dangerous, so I saving money to leave."

"To go to the US?"

"People tell me about America, everybody rich, can make

lots money. Good place for you get education."

"How'd you get out of Hong Kong?"

She broke into the kind of smile a kid might flash after duping the substitute teacher into dismissing the students an hour early. "I call my friend work at travel agency. He help me get tourist visa, have to pay five thousand Hong Kong for that. But can only go to Canada, very hard for America. We take Philippines Airline, can stop in San Francisco. Only can stay ten days. I not want go to Canada. I not know nobody there, but have to go. I ask my brother in San Francisco to help."

"Wait a minute; you have a brother in San Francisco?"

"He die four years ago."

"How come you never told me about him?"

"I tell you, but you not remember." She shot me a scolding stare. "He run away from China before me. I try find him first, but he go to Taiwan."

"What did he do?"

"He manager for factory there, make guns for government, very important." Her voice, clear and direct, affirmed the depth of her feelings for him. "My niece, Ping, you remember her?"

I nodded, afraid not to.

"She marry to Chinese American, so she sponsor my brother go to America. He working for agency help people from another country find job."

"Why didn't he sponsor you to enter the US?"

She shook her head. "No can do. He not citizen."

"What about your niece, the one who sponsored him?"

"*Aiya!* You not know, hah. Must be mother, father, sister, brother. Son, daughter okay. Or husband, wife. Cousin, niece no can do. My brother, he find friend for us to stay in Vancou-vah. We go there from San Francisco, and I working at sewing machine factory eight months, make clothes. I keeping apply to America immigration to visit San Francisco again, but America not want people come stay, so they keeping say no. My brother, he have to write letter for immigration to say he want me come visit him."

"It really happened like this?"

"'Course. You think I make joke?" Her grave expression left no doubt. "America immigration give us two months for visit. My brother help me apply extension for three months more, but I really scared. He think maybe we have to go back."

"So what did you do?"

My mom looked down.

Why did she appear so solemn? Then it hit me full and hard, like a kick to the gut—my stepfather. "Roger?" I said.

She nodded.

"Why didn't you ever tell me?"

"We live with him. I tell you, not fair to him. I tell you, you not see him as father, maybe you not respect."

"He was never my father."

"He try. He drinking too much is all."

"He didn't drink too much for Michael."

We sat still in the darkened corner of the room.

I broke the silence. "How did you meet?"

"I find job as waitress for coffee shop in San Francisco." Her face twisted into a frown. "The owner there Chinese. He very mean, pay little bit. I learn some English in Hong Kong, but my English not good, so he always calling me stupid. He not want use Chinese so talking very fast and say why I not understand?" She chopped the air as if to strike at the memory of her former boss. "Roger come in to eat, and we talk."

"You understood each other?"

"Not so much, but he keeping talking to me. He very patient, teach me some words. He helping me a lot."

Was this the same man who once threatened to set fire to the garage if she bought one more piece of used furniture? "Did he drink?"

"He drink beer, not so much, but he do. He tell me he going to stop if I marry him."

I pictured a graveyard of broken vows swamped in the refuse of shattered beer bottles. "Would you have married him if you already had permanent residency?"

She hesitated. "I want to go to America. My brother there, life better there. I never want to go to Canada, but no choice."

No choice. She remained with this man for twenty-eight years. She cooked, managed their finances, worked and worked more, took care of him, diluting his whiskey bottles with water while he slept. She endured his binges, his lengthy overseas deployments, his refusal to have her friends or relatives over because he didn't want "strange people" in the house, the demeaning barbs about anything Chinese, the endless fighting. She even took him back after his affairs, believing his empty vows to remain faithful.

Would she ever know the feeling of being with a man she respected? A husband she could trust? Someone who could love her?

And what about her children? This was my first trip back to Hong Kong. Michael and Renee had shown little interest in the Far East. They didn't even look Asian. None of us spoke Chinese. None of us wanted to. How did my mother feel knowing her children had abandoned her culture and language, knowing her kids had relatives they might never be able to talk to?

How did she feel taking me from my father?

My mother said, "Roger want to marry me. What I can do? His ship go to San Diego. He not know if Navy let him come back San Francisco, so he want me meeting him in Las Vegas get marry."

"Where was I?"

"Roger and I go to San Diego first. You stay with Ping in San Francisco. We tell her send you to San Diego by airplane."

That was why I had flown by myself as a child. She needed to go alone to San Diego to finalize a Vegas wedding. Too much at stake to jeopardize it with a tag-along.

My mind was spinning, teetering, approaching the point of meltdown. "I'm kind of tired. I think I should get some sleep," I said.

My mother nodded, got up, and went into the kitchen. I heard the glass clink on the counter. Then she walked through the living room. She paused at the bedroom doorway, as if wanting to turn to say something. After a moment she continued into her room and closed the door behind her. The light went off.

Truth 真相

Chapter 8

My mom and I waited with Aunt Poi Yee and her
children at a bus stop to head to an amusement park. My
uncle was at work, and we rode for free only if he came with
us, so when the transport arrived, my aunt reached into
her change purse for fare. I tried to reimburse her, but she
wouldn't allow it.

The air outside clung like a wet sheet. The mugginess
made it hard to walk, and it was a relief to get on the air-
conditioned bus. I didn't know until later that Aunt Poi Yee
paid extra for this luxury on our behalf.

She sat with my mother, while my cousins and I occupied
a bench seat behind them. Ming initiated a game of "rock,
paper, scissors" with Jing-Wei, bursting into laughter
whenever he won. Jing-Wei pouted and complained but kept
battling him with a focused determination. I envied them,
their exuberant play, the close-knit family, a stable home,
parents who didn't go away.

My childhood could not have been more different.
Roger had served in the Navy, spending long months at sea,
and he was restationed at every turn. In the first four and
a half years with Roger, we moved three times, and I lost
my friends. I felt like a foster child sent to a random list of
orphanages.

Being the only Asian at a new school didn't help. The
taunting always began with the same questions: *"Why are your*

eyes like that? How come you people don't eat with a fork? Do you know karate?" If I couldn't demonstrate my proficiency by chopping through a tetherball pole with my bare hands, they would start in, *"Chi-nese . . . Jap-a-nese . . . Dir-ty knees . . . Look at these!"* They'd pull the corners of their eyes to make them slanted. *"Ha! Ha! Ha!"*

Once, a punk in the middle-school quad came up from behind and slapped the side of my head without provocation. I stood there, my face inflamed and throbbing as if someone had pressed a scalding iron against it. But what brought the greatest shame were the looks in the other kids' eyes when I didn't have the courage to retaliate.

Ming thrust out a fist, his "rock" smashing Jing-Wei's "scissors." He flung himself back into his seat, pointing and chortling at his sister. She kept pushing his arm away.

I said, "Can I play?"

They peered at me with puzzled expressions.

I formed the rock, paper, and scissors with my hand. Ming leaned forward in anticipation, but Jing-Wei sat back. My squirrelly cousin beat me three straight, celebrating each victory with boisterous cackling.

Another few turns and his sister edged closer. I said, "Come on, Jing-Wei, I won't bite."

She seemed hesitant. As her brother peered at her, I splayed two fingers over his head and pretended to trim his hair. Jing-Wei covered her mouth and broke into a giggling fit.

Ming stared at his sister as if her bolts needed tightening. Then he turned, saw my hand, and jumped out of his seat to get to me.

* * *

We stepped off the bus into what felt like a sauna. A sprawling sign above an entrance depicted a smiling seal in naval garb with the words "Ocean Park" atop Chinese characters. We headed toward the ticket window, where my aunt refused my mom's money and paid our admission. After we entered the park, I said to my mother, "Maybe they'll let us buy lunch."

"I try, but she not let me."

The park was huge. A winding path through flourishing botanical gardens led to a tropical aviary. My cousins spotted birds of every color and size, while I found only a tangle of trees, branches, and leaves.

Beyond the aviary, we came to a building the color of a fresh sunburn. It rested under a pagoda-style roof, and inside, tank after tank of the most exotic and luminous goldfish filled its many rooms.

We walked on. Despite weather perfectly suited for growing fungus, the place was packed like a rock concert. Aunt Poi Yee led us to a wooden walk bridge overlooking a tranquil turtle pond. My mom wiped her forehead with the rolled-up sleeve of her blouse. Though she tried to hide it, her slumped posture and the way she braced herself against the railing made her fatigue apparent.

It could have been the weather or it might have been a sign of age, but whatever the cause, it was strange to see. My mother had always been tireless, managing a restaurant seven days a week while keeping up the house and paying all the bills and even squeezing in trips to swap meets on Saturday mornings before work.

My aunt gave her a towelette to wipe her face and neck.

I went up to my mom and asked, "Are you okay?"

She caught a breath. "Just too hot here. Little rest, I be

okay."

Down below us, turtles perched like statues on boulders.

My mother studied them. "They not real?"

"I think they are."

"Why they not move?"

"It's hot out here."

She gave a half-hearted chuckle. The turtles didn't budge.

Without looking at me my mom said, "Raymond, what you think about what I say last night?"

The question took me by surprise.

She didn't wait. "I tell you lot about my life." She paused. "And Roger."

I thought a moment before speaking. "You said you didn't tell me about Roger because we lived with him."

She nodded.

"But it was okay to tell me here?"

"Now time for you know."

"But not before?"

"You not need know before."

"I didn't need to know?"

"What good for that? If I tell you, you not respect Roger. He your father from when you little boy."

"He's not my father."

"He do his best for you." She gazed into the murky pond.

"He never treated me like his son."

She kept staring at the muddy water. "Maybe you not give him chance. It not so easy for people get close to you. You do that way with me too, but I never try hurt you."

Without another word my mother continued across the bridge.

Outcasts 孤立

Chapter 9

Aunt Poi Yee and her family sat with my mother and me on stools around a square folding table in the living room to enjoy a dinner of steamed rice and stir-fried Chinese mustard greens and shrimp in flavorful, seasoned oil.

Ming, as usual, scarfed his food, while Uncle Chun-Kwok wouldn't let me stop eating. Every time I paused, he would spoon another helping of rice into my bowl and heap on the vegetables and shrimp. I protested, but my mother said, "He say healthy for you eat more."

Spirited conversation accompanied the meal, and I could tell that my mom was discussing the prices of tours to Beijing with my aunt and uncle. Somehow, I felt more at ease listening to them speak a language I could barely understand than I ever did at the dinner table with my mother and stepfather.

When we finished eating, Uncle Chun-Kwok cleared and washed the dishes.

On the futon couch Mom said, "Your uncle really good man. See how he work all day and still helping Poi Yee?"

My mother wasn't around much for Roger to help. When I was in grade school, she started going to garage sales to buy furniture to resell. In my teens, she worked in a Chinese restaurant and skirted around on weekends searching for real estate investments.

Roger drank. He came home from work, headed straight

to the bar for a Wild Turkey and Coke, and went into the living room to read the paper. Later, as I took care of my siblings, he heated up Mom's leftovers from the refrigerator. While we ate at the dining table, my stepfather plopped his plate on a TV tray in front of the television, picked at his food, and downed drinks as if they were his only companions.

When I was in high school, Roger retired from the Navy and joined a private defense contractor. Years after I moved out, my mother told me his company had laid him off. He didn't try to find another job; he kept drinking. He stopped fixing things around the house, mowing the grass, or even tinkering on his prized Austin Healey in the garage. I wanted to encourage him to look for work, take up a hobby, anything, but I didn't know how to talk to him.

It seemed odd that here in Hong Kong, a place so utterly foreign, I felt at home with my uncle's family. I helped my aunt put the table away, then sat on the couch beside my mom. Ming and Jing-Wei batted a sponge ball with plastic tennis rackets in the living room. Aunt Poi Yee, weary of the ball bouncing off the TV or the fish tank, admonished them to go to their shared room. It didn't take long for the ball to come dribbling out, soon to be followed by my cousins.

As I watched Ming hit a volley past Jing-Wei's flailing backhand, I heard the sound of raindrops peppering the roof. I turned to my mother and said, "It's raining."

"Wow, happen so fast?" Her expression conveyed disbelief.

My aunt sat on a stool next to us and spoke. My mom reported, "Sometimes it raining here, no can tell. She say can be hot outside and still raining."

I loved the rain. Serene and pure, it held a cadence, like

music. Though it didn't rain often in San Diego, I recalled sitting on my bed, my legs secure under the covers, and writing to its purposeful beat. Something about the rain and its misty gray sadness brought me closer to my characters. I would be able to see them, touch them, hear them. They spoke to me, confided their secrets as if to a trusted friend, and I would listen, and write.

Quyen once asked me why I wrote. I didn't know how to respond, yet she seemed comfortable with my silence and reflection. It made me want to tell her. In time I looked into Quyen's eyes and said, *"My first creative writing teacher told me that 'writing is discovery.' I think she knew. When I write a story, I learn things about myself, about life and what's important. I'm usually pretty quiet, so it's hard for people to get to know me. It may sound strange, but writing is my way of connecting to the world."*

Quyen's smile told me she understood.

Now I listened to the rain's symphony in Hong Kong, soaking it in. After a time, Jing-Wei swatted a ball onto the couch and Ming ran over to retrieve it. My aunt reprimanded them again.

I took hold of the ball and said, "Hey, Ming, do you have cards?"

He stared at me, uncomprehending.

I pretended to shuffle a deck and his face lit up. He and his sister raced into the bedroom, and I heard the slamming of drawers. Ming hurried out with Jing-Wei right behind. He extended a deck of cards.

I took it and looked for a surface. Jing-Wei retrieved a folding tray and opened it in front of me. Ming brought two stools and my cousins settled in to observe.

With the deck in one hand I said, "Watch carefully. I'm going to show you something truly amazing."

I shuffled and bridged the cards. Ming squealed as if I had pulled a live gerbil out of a glass of milk.

A great audience, I thought. They're already appreciating the act and I haven't even performed the trick.

The children leaned forward. I spread the cards facedown on the tray and, with hands at my temples and my mom translating, called out a jack of hearts. I asked Ming to touch any card, and I picked it up without revealing it. Then I identified the three of clubs and urged Jing-Wei to touch another card. I slipped that card into my hand. I claimed to feel the energy of a six of diamonds and selected a third card. With a magical wave of my fingers I showed them my hand with those exact cards. Ming stood with mouth agape and Jing-Wei's eyes widened to the size of coat buttons.

I learned the trick from a friend named Henry in the fourth grade at China Lake, a naval weapons station in the Mojave Desert where my stepfather had been stationed for three years. Henry did wondrous magic tricks at school. His repertoire included sleight of hand, disappearing coins, mind reading, and a host of other deceptions. He was so good that teachers asked him to perform at class birthday parties. He never disappointed.

Henry had an intense focus and a high, rounded forehead that suggested he was immersed in thought. His formal manner of speech gave the impression of hubris or condescension, something he used to his advantage in performing, but did not endear him to his classmates otherwise. Kids viewed him as a loner and a snob. The fact he loved magic set him apart even further.

I was Chinese. When kids made fun of my flat nose or skinny body, I pretended it didn't bother me. I built an inner fortress, towering and impenetrable, to house my seething anger. Fueled by their taunts, I pushed myself harder, rode my bike faster, kicked a ball farther, ousted them in four square. The activity didn't matter, only beating them.

Because Henry and I were outcasts, he trusted me. He showed me the secrets to a few of his tricks, but only if I crossed my heart and hoped to die that I would never reveal them to anyone. He also made me vow to never, ever do the same trick twice in a row. Maybe silly, but to this day, I've kept my word.

We lost touch after my family moved to San Diego. I've often wondered what became of Henry. It wouldn't have surprised me if he ended up headlining a magic act in Vegas. I could picture him on stage with a flowing black cape, a top hat, bow tie, and a wand in his fingertips, dazzling and befuddling an appreciative crowd with a gallery of elaborate and carefully orchestrated ruses, something he was put on this earth to do.

I shuffled the cards. "How about if we play a game?"

Blank stares from my cousins. I said, "Okay, I'll show you."

I dealt a hand to each and instructed them on the fine art of Crazy Eights. My mother helped to explain the concept of changing suits.

We played, with Ming winning most of the time. The little weasel grasped the game easily and took particular pleasure in defeating his sister. Once, with calculating deliberateness, he changed the suit and couldn't contain himself as Jing-Wei picked card after card, searching in vain for a heart.

Ming won that game, yelping and giggling as his sister sat, arms folded in disgust, her face a portrait of frustration.

I gave her a soft pat on the shoulder. "Don't let it get you down, Jing-Wei. He just got lucky."

Ming didn't make it easier by scooting forward on his stool and snickering.

Her memory proved short in the next game. I was the one going through the deck trying to find a club. All the while she did her best imitation of her brother, clapping and laughing with each card I drew.

I crossed my arms and puffed my lips like a fish. Neither of them took mercy on me as they fell out of their seats with laughter. Then I showed them another trick, and again they watched, mesmerized. In the living room with my cousins serenaded by the gentle patter of the rain outside, I saw Henry in my mind, outfitted in a torn plastic black cape and a crooked, brown, construction paper bow tie, and silently thanked him.

Crossroads 十字路口

Chapter 10

My aunt, her children, my mother, and I toured Hong Kong Park, a plant conservatory featuring a vast array of sparkling fountains and waterfalls. The sky was clear and the air carried the fresh fragrance of nature. We climbed a path next to a wide, blue-tiled stairway fountain with rippling water cascading down its steps. At the top, I could see expansive lush ponds and fields of bright azaleas in pinks, purples, and vibrant yellows.

My mom stopped at a display of gigantic water lilies blooming with white lotus flowers blanketing the surface of a pond. The largest lily measured three times the diameter of a dinner plate, and each presented an outer lip curled toward the sky as if reaching to cup a drink of sunlight. A wedding couple posed for a photographer in front of the water plants.

My mother turned to me and said, "Prob-ly lots people get marry here."

No doubt. The rich greenery and fertile gardens surrounded by soothing fountains and majestic waterfalls produced breathtaking backdrops, and it was one of the few places in Hong Kong that didn't seem overrun with people.

Mom observed the bride in her long, layered, white-lace gown. "Pretty face, slim figure. If tall, very good."

"Slap on a pair of six-inch spike heels and problem solved."

"You keep to writing. Bob Hope have nothing to worry about from you." She remained quiet, then added, "What things you write?"

I hesitated. I had never shared my stories with her. They were personal and they were mine. As a child, I didn't have a lot of things. I didn't own trendy clothes or drive a Datsun 240Z like the more popular teens. I didn't make many friends. I wasn't part of the "in group," the ones who smoked in the bathrooms between classes and drove off campus to terrorize the Del Taco drive-through at lunch.

I went unnoticed and took refuge in my journals. The penciled scribblings inside those dog-eared spiral notebooks were my truest friends, the only ones I could count on.

I looked at my mother and said, "I write different things."

"What kind things?"

"About people."

"Just people?"

Why was this so hard? "They're usually going through some problems."

"You write make it better?"

Did I make the problems better? How to explain that I didn't make them anything? I wasn't a puppeteer dangling words on a string. The people in my stories told their own tales and I learned about life through them.

"Sometimes they get worse."

"Why you write them like that?"

"That's how they come out."

Mom looked puzzled. "What good for that? Spend so much time, what you get?"

I didn't know how to convey it in a way she would understand.

I turned to the wedding couple. With water lilies

flourishing in the background, the groom positioned himself next to his bride and circled his arm around her waist. Tall and dapper in a teal tuxedo, he clasped the white-gloved hand of the woman he would spend the rest of his life with. Rest of his life . . . I pondered the very idea: coming home to the same person day after day, making decisions together, wanting to be with her, knowing that of all the people in the world, she mattered the most.

I was too busy for relationships: college, studying, internship, work, graduate school, more studying, more work. No time. At least that's what I told myself.

Donna came the closest. She was separated, with two kids of her own to take care of. I knew my mother would never accept her. That's what drew me to her.

The memory surfaced like a splintered wreckage at sea. Donna lay next to me on the bed. A faint moonlight edged through the blinds. Neither of us had spoken for a time, as if afraid to. Finally she said, *"This isn't going to work, is it?"*

I stared into darkness.

She continued, *"It's always going to be like this. If I need something from you, you'll do it. That's how you are."* She took a breath. *"But then you'll pull away, because it's not what you really wanted."* Her voice, even, controlled, concealed any trace of emotion.

Silence. Cold and still. Like death. She propped herself up on her elbows. *"Tell me, Ray. At least give me that much."*

I shook my head slowly.

"Do you really want to be with me? Can you be a father to Jonathan and Timothy?"

She waited.

"Ray."

My stepfather's face, flush with contempt, flashed before

me.

I looked at Donna. She peered at me, her eyes searching, pleading for something I didn't know how to give. I saw sadness on her face. Resignation. And pain. Pain I had caused.

Now, my mother's words reverberated in my mind. *"It not so easy for people get close to you. You do that way with me too, but I never try hurt you."*

I stared at the wedding couple, the man's arm around his bride. The click of a camera shutter, this image of the start of their lives together, captured forever.

I turned and began to walk. I didn't look back.

Childhood 童年

Chapter 11

A sharp, intense blue filled the sky. Near the top of
Victoria Peak a huge terrace adjacent to a shopping mall
provided a panoramic view. The ocean's expanse, dotted
with tiny toylike vessels in the distance, combined with
steep, densely treed hillsides in the foreground to paint a
magnificent picture of Hong Kong's towering skyline.

Ming disappeared among dozens of children climbing,
jumping, and tumbling in a jungle gym at one end of
the terrace. They scrambled up steel steps to stomp on a
black rubber platform at the summit of a parallel slide,
whipped down screaming side by side, and ran to ride
atop multicolored cars, each bouncing on a single, shock-
absorbing spring.

Jing-Wei stood by her mom, watching a free-spirited
boy in black shorts and a Superman T-shirt hurtling down a
bumpy slide. My aunt urged her daughter to go play.

My mother said to me, "You do like Jing-Wei when you
little boy, never want to play with other kids."

Spurred by Aunt Poi Yee, Jing-Wei walked toward the
monkey bars. She looked back at my aunt, who waved her
on. At the bars my cousin began a tentative climb.

I walked over to Ming as he jumped on the surface of
the cushiony blue-padded floor near a children's plastic
clubhouse complete with bench seats, a round table, and
attached peak-through crawl tunnel. Ming squirmed into the

tunnel and emerged at the other end to join a group of kids in the clubhouse. He soon came bounding back out.

A short time later I heard my aunt calling to us and turned to see her signaling. Jing-Wei already waited next to her.

I told Ming we needed to go. He said something in a voice of complaint and I pointed to his mother. His sulky, long-drawn face captured the full extent of his disappointment.

We hurried to join the others and made our way through the mall. Aunt Poi Yee directed us up an escalator to another level. After some window browsing we proceeded through a glass door to another terrace that afforded us a sweeping view of the city.

Ming skipped over to a telescope stand and summoned his mother. She reached into her purse, pulled out change, and deposited a coin. She lifted her son to the eyehole.

I reached out and offered to hold Ming for her. She nodded, set her son down, and switched places with me. I circled my arms around Ming's waist and hoisted him. Squinting with one eye, he peered into the lens and aimed the telescope at the buildings, the bay beyond, and up to the sky.

Engrossed, he didn't notice me tightening my grip on him with my left arm and drawing my right hand up to flick his hair.

I felt a tug on my shirt and turned to see Jing-Wei motioning to the telescope. She pleaded with her brother, who acted as if she was urging him to clean his room.

I lowered him to animated, drawn-out protests. When my aunt intervened, he released my arm and slumped away.

Jing-Wei wasted no time in assuming her brother's place,

looking up to indicate her readiness to be raised. I had become a human elevator.

Aunt Poi Yee allowed her daughter a turn at the telescope before leading us to the exit. She conversed with my mom while I engaged in a game of splaying my fingers behind Ming's head before he could see me.

At the door we paused to let a stooped, elderly woman onto the terrace. Her craggy face poked through a russet-brown scarf bundled around her head. She slipped past us in silence, her gray glassy eyes staring straight ahead. That's when I heard a sliding sound followed by a thumping splash from behind.

I whirled to see Jing-Wei sprawled in a puddle. She lay on her back in the middle of the water with a horror-stricken look on her face.

My aunt rushed over to her daughter. She pulled Kleenex out of her purse to dab the moisture on my cousin's neck, arms, and legs. Wads of wet tissues landed everywhere, but Jing-Wei's T-shirt and shorts were soaked.

The old woman in the scarf stood beside the puddle and lectured Jing-Wei in the manner of a football coach whose rookie running back had just lost his fourth fumble of the game. My cousin stood still, her face burning with shame. Aunt Poi Yee kept drying her.

The stranger gestured at the puddle and berated Jing-Wei in a caustic "you should know better" tone of voice. I didn't understand what she was saying, but I felt something searing rising up from the pit of my being, something molten red and raging.

I knew how it felt to be afraid. To be shy. I understood Jing-Wei's fear of drawing attention to herself, of being seen, because being noticed meant you were doing something wrong. Or worse, there was something wrong about you. And it was better to be invisible than ostracized.

Jing-Wei's face had turned pale, her eyes vacant like those of war crime victims. I wanted to help my cousin, but my legs seemed rooted into the ground. My heart drummed inside my chest and my skin went clammy.

I was a child. Voices, loud, the taunts, "*Chin-ese . . . Jap-a-nese . . .*" My humiliation in middle school after the bully smacked my head . . . My mother slapping her hands together in the living room as I watched her shout at Roger. "*You good for nothing, I tell you. Now we have no money. You know that? How we pay the rent? How we eat?*"

My stepfather, sitting on the couch, wouldn't make eye contact with my mom. "*If someone would quit bitchin' all the time, I wouldn't have to go out to get a God damn drink. Don't make a big deal out of this.*"

My mother picked up the bill from the coffee table. "*Big deal? Where the money go, Roger? Tell me where the money go. You take her go drinking, gamble, sleep in hotel? That what you do?*" She staked out a position at the arm of the couch and stood over Roger. Her eyes seemed to bulge out of their sockets as she pointed the bill at him like a knife.

My stepfather shook his head as if the action would somehow banish this woman from his world. He got up and walked away from her toward the kitchen.

My mom chased him down and reached the kitchen cabinet first. "*No, you not drinking here. You want kill yourself.*" She flung open a cupboard and grabbed a tumbler. "*Here, I help you.*" She sprinted to the garage entrance. I heard the door swing open, the sound of her frantic footsteps in the garage.

My stepfather came back into the living room

empty-handed, walked over to the television, and turned it on. Gilligan was calling out to the Skipper. Roger went to the couch and sat to watch TV.

When Mom returned to the kitchen, she held a box of roach poison in one hand and the tumbler in the other. She poured the white powder into his tumbler and reached into the cabinet next to the refrigerator for his whiskey bottle. She filled the tumbler with Wild Turkey and left the bottle and poison on the kitchen counter as if they were ingredients to bake chocolate chip cookies.

My mother ran into the living room with the tumbler, spilling booze and poison along the way. My stepfather observed her approach without a word. She pushed the drink at his face, and he turned away from it. When she spoke, venom dripped from her voice, *"You want drink? Here. Go ahead. Have a drink. Invite your stripper friend too. Go ahead."*

Now I stared at my cousin, stunned and helpless before this woman's onslaught. My clenched fingers dug deep into the palms of my fists. Shaking, I forced myself forward a step at a time until I reached the woman. "Leave her alone," I said, my voice trembling.

She gazed at me with complete incomprehension.

I glared at her. "She's already feeling bad enough. Just leave her alone." My words, steadier, came out low, threatening.

The woman just stood there, her mouth gaping. Then without a sound, and never taking her eyes off me, she circled around me and backed away toward the other side of the terrace.

I turned to Jing-Wei, who held my aunt's hand. My cousin wore the guilt-ridden expression of a child caught ditching.

I walked up to my cousin and said, "Don't worry, Jing-Wei. You didn't do anything wrong."

She looked at me and I'm not sure if she understood.

* * *

We went into a department store, and Aunt Poi Yee bought clothes for her daughter to change into.

In line I said to my mom, "What was that woman going on about?"

"She say Jing-Wei too old to play in water, should stay close by her mother." She added, "Something wrong? I never see you like that before."

"That woman didn't have to say anything. You don't do that to a child."

She regarded me in silence.

Loyalty 忠誠

Chapter 12

On Sunday my mom and I set off to Kowloon to visit one of her relatives. It was less than ten miles away, but she informed me that in the past, people needed to ferry from Hong Kong Island across the bay to get there. Now a tunnel provided land access.

Aunt Poi Yee and my cousins led us to the bus stop where my aunt instructed us. She pointed at the oncoming traffic, then at the bus sign, before checking my mother's change.

Two-tiered buses came and went, leaving a trail of exhaust in their wake. Aunt Poi Yee motioned at an approaching transport to inform the driver to keep going.

My mom said, "We have to be careful because the last bus come back eight o'clock. Have to make sure not to miss, otherwise need to take taxi, very expensive."

"I'm not the one who's always running late."

"You tell me if getting close to eight. Make sure." She counted her coins. "After we there, Poi Yee want me to call her, so she know we okay."

I looked at my aunt. A week ago, I didn't even know the woman. Now I couldn't think of anyone I'd rather have watching over us.

When our bus arrived, she climbed aboard to make sure we deposited the correct fare. She gave my mother a final instruction, waved to us, and turned to step off.

As soon as Aunt Poi Yee was clear, the driver accelerated.

My mom and I grabbed handrails, and I propped my hand on her back to steady her as we shuffled to the rear of the vehicle.

We sat on a bench seat, and it didn't take long for the first electronic ring to signal a call on someone's cellular. I thought California was bad, with every third driver on the freeway yapping into a car phone. What could possibly be important enough to gab about while operating three thousand pounds of barreling steel?

Here, everyone carried a pocket cellular, and it wasn't unusual to hop on a bus with half a dozen phone conversations running.

I said to my mother, "Who are we going to see again?"

"You remember Daaihyih?"

I nodded. As a child I used the Chinese term to refer to my mom's older sister. When my mother and father worked in Hong Kong, Daaihyih took care of me. I recalled her hearty, earnest eyes framed by square, black-rimmed glasses, her warm, soulful smile, and the smell of camphor as she layered ointment onto my back to soothe the effects of a cold.

I still remember the day we received the news about Daaihyih's death from a stroke. It was the only time I ever saw my mom cry.

"We go visit her son, Lau. He do very good working for lawyer. He have two sons younger than you. They very smart. One engineer, one study pharmacy." She paused and fixed a steely gaze on me, the kind insinuating the worthiness of *their* chosen professions. "Lau speak English and Chinese too, very smart."

Again the use of the word "smart." My mother put a premium on intelligence, associating it with schooling, success, and wealth, quantifiable measures of a person's accomplishments in life.

I possessed a master's degree in counseling that didn't merit praise. To her, if I had made full use of my faculties, I would've majored in business or gone to medical school to pursue a career that could provide for my eventual wife and family and earn a title she could discuss proudly with her relatives. Include the fact that I worked with "lazy people" for low pay, and in my mother's eyes, I had selected the curtain with the mule behind it from Monty Hall.

"I never knew your sister had a son."

"I tell you before."

She probably did, but "Recall of Chinese Relatives" never qualified as my strongest subject.

"She the one I borrow money to buy house in Hong Kong, the one Uncle Chun-Kwok stay?"

"Right."

"I have older brother too, the one I tell you—"

"In San Francisco."

"Good. They both older than me. They from my father's number one wife."

"Your father's number one wife?"

"Yes, my father marry to another woman before. Wife Number One die when my father forty-six. He not marry to my mother until he fifty-two."

"You never told me that."

"Happen all the time. Someone die, find somebody else. In China, used to be if man have lots money, can have more than one wife."

"This was accepted?"

"That the past."

"How did you feel about Daaihyih having a different

mother? Did it affect your relationship with her?"

"She my sister; we very close. She take good care for you."

A few rows ahead of us, a woman reprimanded a boy Ming's age for snatching a plastic harmonica from a younger, puffy-cheeked girl next to him. "Did Daaihyih come to Hong Kong first?"

My mom paused; the lines in her brow dipped in the strains of deep concentration. "She marry to man in China, Lau's father. Her husband do business in America, so he go often. His mother very sick, so Daaihyih stay in China, because the tradition for wife take care the husband's parents."

"He went to another country, and she remained behind?"

"No choice. Have to be. The husband send money for her, but he . . . he meet American woman." Her voice grew solemn and she looked away from me. "They get marry."

"How could he do that?"

"In China before, people get marry, they have big party, invite all the friends and relatives. They sign card, red color, to witnessing. The man, woman pray like this." She put her palms together, fingers pointing to the ceiling of the bus. "That all. No license, no paper, nothing. You go to another country, get marry, nobody know."

"So what did Daaihyih do?"

"She take care the mother."

"Even after her husband left her?"

Mom nodded.

"Did she ever remarry?"

"She never feel right to do that."

"So she thought he was going to come back?"

My mother shook her head.

"Then why?"

"That the way she think is right." There was softness in my mom's voice, in her eyes, a kind of knowing, as if she understood her sister's motivation, understood it well, and respected her for it.

And right then I realized how my mom could stay married all these years to a man who had long ago abandoned her for a bottle.

Caring 關懷

Chapter 13

Ming's finger traced the sentences in a picture book. "Jim is at the park. He like to—"

"Likes. Jim likes to play." I underlined the *s* with my finger.

"Jim is at the park. He likes to play with his mother and si— si—"

"Sound it out."

"Sis-ter."

"Good."

My cousin beamed. As he continued reading, the phone rang. He leaped off the couch, scrambled to the phone on the counter, and grabbed it before Jing-Wei could.

He held an earpiece as long as his face and said, "*Wei.*"

As Ming listened, his cheeks curled into a grin, and an animated excitement shone in his eyes.

Moments later he dropped the earpiece on the counter with a loud clack and raced to my mother's door. He knocked and called to her.

Mom came out and went to the phone. She spoke briefly, hung up, and looked at me. "That your father. He say he want us go to China tomorrow." She said it in an even voice.

"You feel okay with this?"

She nodded and spoke to my aunt.

Ming, who scooted beside me on the couch again, pulled on my sleeve to indicate his eagerness to commence reading.

Jing-Wei observed us.

Aunt Poi Yee made an announcement and my cousins hurried off to their room.

My mother reported, "She say we get ready go to beach."

* * *

We took the bus to Deep Water Bay on the southern tip of Hong Kong Island. Most of the beachgoers gathered in a half-mile stretch of sand rimmed by a hillside of tall, modern buildings. Children played in shallow water, and older swimmers waded farther out between three large drum decks floating a hundred feet apart. Youths launched themselves from the bobbing surfaces and descended with an exuberant scream into a loud splash.

This bay was different from San Diego beaches. Most women wore one-piece bathing suits instead of the neon-bright thong and string bikinis seen in Southern California. Here the emphasis seemed more on having fun with family and friends than auditioning for the latest Coppertone commercial.

My aunt found a spot and spread a blanket on the sand. She used a hand pump to inflate two inner tubes. Aunt Poi Yee slipped one on each of my cousins and strapped goggles on their heads. My cousins stood with inner tubes hugging their tummies, and I couldn't suppress a chuckle at the image of rotund, pint-sized, bug-eyed aliens preparing to tiptoe into a swamp.

My aunt spoke to my mother, who said, "She ask if you know how to swim."

I stroked my arms like Mark Spitz. After Aunt Poi Yee issued instructions, Ming and Jing-Wei sprinted giggling toward the water.

I pulled off my T-shirt and turned to my mom and aunt. "Are you two going in?"

"You go. We okay here."

I jogged to the bay's edge and braced myself. In San Diego, I dreaded the ocean's chilling bite and would try to delay it by stepping in slowly. Only when the icy coldness crept its way up to the bottoms of my trunks would I end the torture by doing a headfirst dive into an oncoming wave.

Here I encountered the peculiar sensation of warm ripples washing over my feet. It felt like a heated pool!

Around me kids shouted and splashed. A spindly man, with a chest shaped like the inside of a bowl, trudged through waist-high water with a child straddling his shoulders. My cousins floated twenty feet ahead, dog-paddling. I took a deep breath and knifed into the dark and murky depths. Unable to see more than a few yards ahead, I surfaced and swam toward my cousins. With each breath I tasted saltwater.

I caught up and Ming, copying my swimming motion, let out a delighted shriek. His churning arms deluged me in spray.

I submerged, slipped past him, and came up splashing. Jing-Wei wasted no time in helping her brother.

Outnumbered, I sought refuge. At one of the decks a young woman in a fuchsia floral swimsuit climbed a metal ladder while a small group sunbathed on the rubber platform. Teens executed leaping cannonball plunges into the bay from running starts.

I swam to the deck's ladder and hoisted myself onto a swaying surface that spanned twenty feet in diameter. The air didn't feel cold, and for once, I was actually grateful for the Hong Kong humidity.

Gazing out, I saw the tiny figures of my mom and aunt

in the background. I was about to wave when a piercing cry stopped my hand in mid-ascent. Fifty feet from the drum, Ming was screaming and flailing in apparent agony.

I ran to the edge of the deck, dove into the water, and swam toward him. What could've happened? Was he bitten or stung by something? Did his inner tube pop? Cramps? Worse?

My arms ripped through the water, my legs kicking hard. It took an eternity to cover the distance. I prayed that it wasn't something serious. At least a hundred yards from the shore, I didn't know how fast I could get him there. I reached him and grasped his arm. "What is it, Ming? Are you hurt?"

He looked at me, his face serious for a second. Then he broke out in raucous laughter.

Thoughts of murder flashed through my mind. I clutched his bony shoulders, and it took every ounce of my willpower to stop me from dunking him.

"Ming, don't you ever do that again, do you hear me?"

Either the volume of my voice or the stony glare I fixed on him brought an abrupt end to his laughter.

"Come on, we're going back." I gestured to the shore.

Without a word, he started paddling in that direction. Jing-Wei followed him.

Neither of them spoke as I swam behind them all the way in.

Once we arrived at the blanket, my mother said, "You done already?"

"Yeah."

She studied me. "Something wrong?"

"No. I've had enough swimming for today, that's all."

* * *

On the bus, Ming, who sat with his family in front of us, kept craning to look at me.

My mom said, "You quiet since we go to beach."

I said, "Ming pretended to be hurt in the water. I thought something was wrong."

"It make you upset?"

I nodded.

"Maybe you care about somebody a lot make you upset. Sometimes happen like that."

I regarded her.

When she spoke next, it was to Ming. After a quick exchange between them, she said to me, "I tell him not to play like that because people think he need help."

He uttered something barely audible.

"He want me tell you sorry, and he not do again."

My cousin watched me. I reached out and ruffled his hair. I said, "I was just concerned about you."

He smiled and turned to splay two fingers behind Jing-Wei's head.

Family 家庭

Chapter 14

After dinner I tried to help Uncle Chun-Kwok with the dishes, but his refusal was as steadfast as my aunt's had been in accepting money from us. I went back into the living room to relax on the futon couch beside my mom. She talked to Aunt Poi Yee, who sat on a stool near us. Soon my uncle came out from the kitchen and pulled up a stool next to his wife.

Jing-Wei stood by the aquarium, trying to juggle a pair of balled-up socks. Ming rolled a plastic yellow bus along the counter by the TV and made chugging engine sounds.

My aunt spoke and my mother translated. "She say Ming do like Uncle. On the bus, he always know where it go. Even when Uncle not with them, Ming know."

Uncle Chun-Kwok responded to Aunt Poi Yee and the two entered into an earnest conversation.

My mom said in a quiet voice, "He not want Ming or Jing-Wei drive bus. He say good money, but very hard job. He want them go college."

My aunt and uncle were talking about their children's future, something I never recalled my parents doing. My stepfather didn't interfere in my decisions, but my mother's attempts to coax me into a high-profile profession with high-profile pay came across as so much meddling. My attitude: let me live my own life.

I asked Mom if she agreed with my uncle.

"He know. He drive bus for long time, so he want something better for his kids."

I wondered if she ever held that type of discussion with my father. Did they ever contemplate my future? Imagine the career I would enter? Plan for my education? The thoughts—a littered stream of discarded fantasies—took me to a place of sorrow and emptiness.

In time Ming and Jing-Wei started a jigsaw puzzle at a folding table. Uncle Chun-Kwok spoke to my mother and beckoned her to follow him. She turned to me and said, "He want to show me some antiques in the other house. We be right back."

I nodded and they walked out the door.

My cousins were absorbed in the puzzle. I peeked over their shoulders and could make out a tar-thatched barn roof and the beginnings of a horse stable.

I looked at my aunt, who smiled. I said, "You have a wonderful family."

Her expression didn't change.

I pointed to her, then my cousins. "Nice, good."

Ming watched us.

Aunt Poi Yee nodded and pointed at me. "Goot." Then she touched her wedding band and motioned to her children and back to me. "Goot."

I shook my head. "That's hard for me to imagine."

She spoke in a sincere voice while pushing her hands toward me as if to usher a baby to his first steps. She said, "Goot."

I smiled and said, "*Dojeh.*" Remembering how my mom told me to address an aunt, I added, "*Dojeh,* A-sam."

Her face registered a delighted surprise.

Though we spoke different languages, I never felt

awkward around Aunt Poi Yee. Her calm and nurturing presence made me glad my uncle married her, that Ming and Jing-Wei would always feel secure in her love and guidance.

I looked up at the black-and-white portrait of a man with earnest, penetrating eyes on the pedestal above the TV. "A-sam, who's that?"

She followed my gaze. She touched her sternum. "Ah, ma-ma," She shook her head and suggested someone tall with her hand.

"Your father? That's your father?"

She nodded.

"He looks like a very wise man. Very good."

She seemed pleased that I asked about him. In a moment she pointed to the picture and said, "Fa-da, goot," and to me. "You, fa-da, goot."

I smiled.

"*Sik teng?*"

"*Sik.*" I understood.

Ming got up, went to his room, and brought out a pocket-sized photo album. He scooted beside me and thrust the book onto my lap. I opened it to a full-page photograph of an infant swaddled in a yellow blanket and wearing a snug, white knit cap. The baby's provocative eyes could only belong to Ming.

The next picture portrayed Aunt Poi Yee, with longer, shoulder-length hair, snuggling the little tot on the couch in this room. Then a shot of my cousin on Uncle Chun-Kwok's lap by the aquarium.

"How old were you here, Ming?"

He stared at me.

"How old?" I held up a finger, then two.

He extended his index finger.

I said, "One."

He repeated, "One."

I patted his head. "Just a little pup."

In the photos I saw my cousin at every age: with his father in the kitchen, on the redbrick steps in front of his school, birthday parties, a stage showcasing a Captain Hook costumed Ming wielding a plastic saber, next to his sister at Ocean Park, the whole family on a beach blanket at Deep Water Bay. I was watching him grow up.

I paused at a picture of him sitting on the couch by a middle-aged woman bearing an unmistakable resemblance to Aunt Poi Yee.

"Ming, who's this?"

He pointed to his mom. I showed her and she outlined someone tall with her hands. She said, "*Gaje.*"

"Older sister?"

Ming tapped my arm and said, "*Haih,* sister."

"Ming, that's your aunt!"

He said, "Aunt."

"That's right. You have an aunt and I have one, too." I gazed at Aunt Poi Yee, who smiled her acknowledgment.

Jing-Wei went into the bedroom, brought out her own album, and waited her turn. In Jing-Wei's baby pictures, I noticed my uncle's fuller hair. The dome of his forehead wasn't so pronounced. When he and his wife cuddled their tiny daughter, their faces gleamed with the unbridled joy of new parents.

As I examined a photo of Jing-Wei in pink baby cap and matching mittens, Uncle Chun-Kwok and my mom entered the house.

She hurried to me and reported, "Uncle say your father

give him money to buy clothes for you, but you not let him buy, so he give money for you take go to China."

She extended a roll of Hong Kong hundred-dollar notes.

I glanced at the bills. Then I said, "You know, they've spent a lot on us, taking us everywhere, food, taxis, all the bus rides. Plus they're letting us stay here. Why don't we let them keep it?"

She opened her mouth to speak, stopped herself. She tried to return the cash to Uncle Chun-Kwok.

He waved her away, chastising her as if she were a belligerent child. She moved toward him again, and he stepped back, brushing her arm aside.

She said to me, "He say money not belong to him, he not want."

"Tell him he should keep it for his family because they've done so much for us."

She did and my aunt came to me and said, "Fada for you." She spoke with unwavering certainty, her eyes peering into mine. She motioned to the money in my mother's hand and tapped my chest as if to drum some sense into me.

I looked at her, my uncle, and then my mom, unsure of what to do.

Uncle Chun-Kwok issued a statement in a voice which brooked no argument.

Aunt Poi Yee added her support in the same firm tone.

"They say you too much concerned. The money from your father for you, not for them. They say you not have to worry about them. They let you stay, take care of you because you the family. That how Chinese people do."

My uncle spoke again, gesturing to Ming and Jing-Wei.

"He say he hope you see them like that. Someday, they come visit you, you taking care for them. Maybe you help

Ming and Jing-Wei. He hope they not have to make sure count money for that."

I regarded my uncle for a moment, then my aunt. Both my cousins watched me.

I turned to Uncle Chun-Kwok. "When you come to visit me in San Diego, I'll take care of all of you. And you won't have to worry about paying me back, because you're my family." I looked at Aunt Poi Yee and said, "I won't ever forget that."

China 中國

Chapter 15

My father and Uncle Number One's son, Hoy, accompanied my mother and me on the hourlong train ride. Skyscrapers and congested streets had given way to flat, open country. We skirted long stretches of rice fields and vast plains, and patches of scraggly, gnarled-limbed trees pocketed the landscape.

I turned to my mom beside me and asked, "Who are we seeing again?"

"We go visit your uncles in Canton. Number One have house. Number Two, Number Four, maybe they come visit."

"What about Number Three?"

She shot me a scathing look. "Your father Number Three."

"Oh." A moment later I said, "Number Six is Uncle Chun-Kwok, and Number Seven's the one who talks a lot."

Surprise surfaced on her face. Then she nodded. "Number Five die last year."

"What happened to him?" I asked.

She shrugged. "I not hear yet, but maybe they say something later."

My mom's uncanny knack for obtaining information: after she introduced me to customers at her restaurant and when we were safely out of earshot, she would recite their education, occupation, marital status, major accomplishments, the size of their house, number of children, and

usually a defining characteristic such as a teenage son in
drug rehab. The amazing thing—and I witnessed this on
many occasions—she asked the most personal questions and
they answered!

Not me. I tended to keep things to myself, but more
so with my mother. I had seen her torpedo my stepfather
with information he freely provided. Her aim, always true,
resulted in the target's surrender, or annihilation.

"Your father ask what you think about Hong Kong." My
mom's voice jarred me from my thoughts. I looked across
the aisle at my father.

"It's different from America, the people, the customs,
everything. It's kind of overwhelming," I said.

She translated and he spoke again.

"He say sorry he not have enough room for us. He ask if
okay for you stay with Uncle."

I gazed at my father. "You don't have to apologize. It's
been wonderful staying with your brother's family."

As she relayed this, he smiled. A moment later he posed
another question.

"He say you thirty-three. Do you get marry soon?" My
mother trained her eyes on me.

"I don't know about that," I said.

Hoy, cheeks drawn into a devious smile, commented. He
gestured to me and his booming voice drew the attention of
nearby passengers.

Mom responded as if he had insulted her taste in living
room furniture. A disquieting feeling accompanied the fact
that my Chinese name kept popping up in their debate.
After listening to their interminable argument for as long
as I could stand, I said to my mother, "What are you talking
about?"

She looked at me, to Hoy briefly, and back to me. "Hoy crazy. He say you still young, should go out, have fun before get marry. He say life short, have to enjoy. I think he loco."

Hoy flashed a gaping grin, giving me the thumbs up with his thick hand.

I shrugged.

He nodded at me and said something in a tone rife with conspiracy.

Mom swiped the air as if trying to repel mosquitoes.

Hoy didn't let up. He kept egging me on, as if I understood his every word.

My mother reprimanded Hoy again, and he splayed his hands wide, palms raised in a pose I could picture him using at an arraignment hearing. In a point-blank interrogation befitting a prosecuting attorney, she pressed her attack— short sentences slamming the opposition in rapid succession so as not to allow rebuttal.

To his credit, Hoy seemed to manage some deft sidesteps, squeezing in a few retorts.

My father watched in silence.

The combatants continued, moving ahead, I suspected, to philosophical and value differences unrelated to my relationships with the opposite sex. The glint in Hoy's eyes told me he was in his element. He goaded her, leaning forward to speak in loud, short sentences, then lounged back in his seat, smiling in silence as he waited for her reply. Mom retaliated with her bludgeoning force of will and I wondered if Hoy realized what he was up against. They were still at it when the train came to a halt. If my father hadn't called their attention to this, they might've battled right through our stop.

As if the fray with my mother amounted to nothing

more than chitchat, Hoy lifted the two bags from under his seat and proceeded to an exit.

Once off the train we walked through a station much different from the one in Hong Kong. Here, barren stone walls, absent of billboards or advertisements, surrounded us. The signs above displayed only Chinese characters. The empty walls and concrete floor didn't extend a warm greeting—just the opposite, I felt a palpable trepidation.

I looked at my mom, who stayed silent. Did an unsettling tension grip her as well?

We followed the wave of people through a long corridor and climbed a set of stairs to another hallway. My father stopped at a counter and tore off four sheets of Chinese-printed paper from a pad. He gave one to each of us, but I saw nothing to write with on the counter. My mother reached into her purse for a pen and filled in her document and mine, her hands fashioning Chinese characters with ease. I asked about the forms.

"Arrival papers, like the ones in Hong Kong," she said and handed one to me. I folded and inserted it into my travel belt.

We started forward. My mom surveyed the surroundings and said, "Have to be more careful here. Uncle tell me that China even more dangerous than Hong Kong."

Three lines formed ahead. Hoy and my father went to one, my mother and I to another. I set the travel bag down. Mom peered at it, so I reached for the strap.

She said, "Prob-ly check the passports here."

I looked around, and people averted their gazes. Why had they been staring? Then it registered. We were Chinese people communicating in English. My mother once hired a waiter, an American student with military-length, reddish-blond hair and a youthful face that reminded me of Ron Howard. The guy studied Chinese and often traveled to Hong Kong. When I ate lunch at the restaurant, the new waiter served me. My mom, ringing up tickets at the cash register, gave him instructions in Cantonese. He responded in kind! There aren't many sights stranger than a Caucasian face vocalizing Chinese sounds and inflections. My mother went out of her way to speak loudly and often to him while I could only gawk in amazement.

In the center line, travelers carried department store bags stuffed with merchandise. Some lugged packages of clothing, boxed candies, dried fruit, and even carts containing small appliances and stereo equipment. An old, hunched man supported two heaped baskets on the ends of a bamboo pole across his shoulders.

I asked my mom, "Why are they taking so many things to China?"

"Some people not often get chance go to Hong Kong, so they bring back a lot for family," she said.

At the front, a soldier wearing an olive-green uniform and hat stood ramrod straight next to the man inspecting passports. His hat displayed a red star against a gold leaf-cluster insignia. Red stripes ran down the sides of his tight-pressed pants, and a holster attached to the thick black belt at his waist held a handgun.

Unlike the Hong Kong airport, the man checking passports here didn't have the benefit of protective glass. He stood at a simple wooden podium with no computer console, yet the guard stationed by him posed a more formidable obstacle than anything in Hong Kong.

The visa inspector studied each person as if fitting him for a uniform. He thumbed through the individual pages of the passport, stamped it with force, and handed it back in an abrupt and firm dismissal.

The checkpoint consisted of a chrome metal gate. Instead of a turnstile, a section of the bars swung forward to allow entry. My mother passed through without incident, and to my relief, I did too. Beyond it I glanced back at the soldier. He stood impassive, his face betraying no hint of emotion.

Hoy and my father waited for us, and my mom spoke to them in a serious tone. They nodded. We continued down a series of long, endless corridors. The concrete floor, a shade darker than the walls, added to the sensation of marching in a dungeon.

At an intersection of hallways a man wearing overalls the color of mold sloshed soapy water along the cement with a mop. No signs warned of a wet floor and I recalled how Jing-Wei slipped in the puddle on the terrace at Victoria Peak. People trudged through, creating a dirty, swishy trail of footprints.

I saw a set of restrooms. "Hang on a minute, Mom. I'm gonna use the bathroom."

She relayed this and said to me, "You leave bag with them. I need use, too."

She went to the door depicting a small figure wearing a triangle-shaped dress and I entered the one with a straight stick figure. The smell of industrial-strength ammonia didn't disguise the odor of urine. I held my breath. The stone floor and walls without mirrors matched the exterior decor. Three sinks with rusty faucets extended from the far end of the restroom. Adjacent to them stood four enclosed stalls. I lifted a door's corroded metal handle and opened it to discover a tiny, sunken cement floor basin. No toilet or tank.

Maybe this was a urinal. I checked the adjoining stall and encountered the same thing. And so with the next. All of them were like that! A hole in the ground was fine if a guy wanted to take a leak, but what if he had more pressing business? Where to sit? I released the breath I had been holding and inhaled through my mouth. A hole. What in the world?

It reminded me of high school math when I attempted to solve the schematic with forty-two broken-lined flaps, the one I needed to fold into a four-dimensional, obtuse, equilateral parahexagram.

I contemplated the basin a while longer and decided the problem was beyond my powers of analytical reasoning. I walked out of the stall and exited the bathroom. My mother already stood with Hoy and my father. I went to them and slung my travel bag on my shoulder. As we proceeded onward, I whispered to my mom, "Did everything go okay in there?"

"What you mean?"

"You know, in the bathroom?"

She looked at me as if I had been guzzling cheap bourbon straight from the bottle.

"Did anything seem kind of strange to you in there?"

Then recognition appeared in her eyes and she let out a laugh. She said, "Many bathrooms like that in China. Even in Hong Kong, some like that." She chuckled again.

At least one of us could see the humor. "Well, how are you supposed to use a toilet with no seat?"

"Have to bend down."

It didn't create a pretty picture in my mind. "I didn't see anywhere to hang up my pants."

She couldn't contain herself as fits of laughter spilled

forth. She was going at it so good tears welled up in her eyes and trickled down her cheeks. She wiped her face. "You not take pants off. You put down by your leg and bend to use."

The picture didn't get any prettier. "That hole in the ground wasn't very big. What if I miss?"

More laughter. "You try your best."

Fabulous. I'd expected to experience new things on this trip, but potty training wasn't one of them.

"You need go back?"

The image played in my head again. "No, I'll wait."

We strode down cement stairs to an area that reminded me of the border between Tijuana and San Diego. A wide, tarred road, blotched with dirt and sand, stretched in front of us. No lane lines, but grungy cars, old platform trucks with wooden crate beds, and flimsy bicycles traveled on the right half of the street.

A squadron of red taxis formed lines in both directions in the middle of the road, making it necessary for pedestrians to brave the journey across to hail a cab. Clear to the other side of the strip—a good hundred feet wide— merchants sold goods at cluttered stands underneath faded canopies.

It was filthy here. Dust and grime caked the streets and sidewalks. Even the air smelled dirty.

And it was hot. The intense, unyielding late-afternoon sun blanketed the earth in an arid heat reminding me of the Mojave Desert.

No towering buildings loomed over us. Only naked dirt fields, dry grass, brush, and a few desolate trees dotting the horizon.

Sweat poured down my legs and I cursed myself for wearing jeans. The three of us waited at a curb littered with empty wrappers and cigarette cartons while my father waded into the street toward the taxis.

The bag on my shoulder felt as though it contained boulders. I dropped it at my feet.

At the center of the road my father talked to a cab driver who dangled a cigarette from the corner of his mouth. After a discussion my father went to another taxi. Seeing this, Hoy put down his bags and jogged over to help.

Three drivers later, the pair returned. My father conveyed something to my mom and she said to me in a tone of unconcealed indifference, "We follow them."

We gathered our bags and headed in the other direction. I climbed the stairs and felt the sweat on my legs seep down to my socks. The boulders in my travel bag were getting larger by the minute.

On the steps an asphalt strip running through the middle allowed pedestrians to roll their luggage on the stairs. I rued the fact that none of our bags had wheels.

At the top I caught my breath and said to my mother, "Why are we going back?"

"He say the taxis not want to take us. Where we go too close for them."

Exasperated, I asked, "You mean they won't accept our money because they're waiting for people who need to go farther?"

She shrugged. "That what he say."

"That's ridiculous. How can they refuse a fare? They could just take us and come back."

"Maybe they lose place in line for more money."

"I thought this was a Communist government. Money's not supposed to be that important."

"You tell them."

We retraced our route through the dungeon's maze of corridors to the bathrooms.

As we approached them my mom said, "You need use? I not know how long before you have another chance."

"No," I said, crossly.

Beyond the restrooms we came to another set of stairs. They led down to a huge parking garage that trapped the heat like a coal-burning engine room. A dozen people waited at a curb as an arc of red taxis circled down a ramp to pick them up.

We got in line behind an elderly woman wearing an old-style, loose-fitting, gray tunic top and pants. My father signaled for me to drop my bag and I unloaded it on the dirty concrete. Only when my father spoke to him did Hoy relinquish the bag from his strong shoulders. He must've been Hong Kong's version of Arnold Schwarzenegger. At least the moistness at his brow indicated he wasn't a machine.

A cab with squealing brakes pulled up to a guy in a business suit. With sweat drenching my polo shirt and jeans I couldn't fathom wearing a coat and tie. We dragged our bags along in the line.

My mother said, "See that in the taxi? More dangerous here than Hong Kong."

Two steel mesh screens closeted the driver from passengers.

I placed a hand on my travel pouch and bent down to get my bag.

"Are these taxis different from the ones outside?"

"Hope so."

One after another they edged up to the curb and drivers negotiated with customers at the head of the line.

A cab inched forward and the woman ahead of us

wheeled her bags on a small steel basket to the passenger door. A brief discussion ensued and the driver waved her in.

She lifted the door handle, but it wouldn't open. Hoy went to help yank on the latch. It didn't budge. Horns blared as he shook the handle and banged on the door. The driver got out and approached them. He tried with similar results and the whole place sounded like a New York City traffic jam.

The man tugged on the handle as irate drivers shouted and honked at him. The noise echoed throughout the parking structure.

Finally, the driver entered his taxi and moved it out of the way. The woman took another cab and my father spoke to the driver of the one behind her. I was relieved when my father called for us.

Hoy loaded our luggage in the trunk and climbed into the front seat. I sat in the rear between my mother and father. We started forward and I caught a glimpse of the other driver working on his passenger door with a screwdriver.

As we exited the station Hoy spoke to the driver. I turned to my mom. "Where are we?"

"This Shenzhen. We in China, but close by Hong Kong."

"This is where my father's family is?"

She shrugged. "All I know is hot here."

Either the taxi didn't have air-conditioning or the driver didn't want to use it, because the windows were down. Hot wind whipped against us as we entered the city.

Contrast 對比

Chapter 16

Shenzhen presented a dichotomy. Parts of the city showcased the commercial buildings, hotels, congested traffic, and expanding population of an emerging metropolis, while outlying rural pockets reminded me of a township in the American Midwest: dirt roads, old single-level dwellings that looked as if the owners couldn't afford the needed repairs, and small shops with loose-planked steps leading up to covered, wood-shingled porches. People rode bicycles with rusty metal baskets to carry groceries, and pedestrians shielded themselves from the scorching sun with umbrellas. The proliferation of grays, browns, and dark hues in the clothing made me feel as if I had been transported into a grainy, black-and-white photograph in a history text.

The taxi took us into a dense, more urban section of the city, and our driver dropped us off at a tenement next to a corroded metal trash bin filled with garbage. My father and Hoy led my mother and me up five flights of stairs to meet Uncle Number Seven and his three children at a tiny, run-down, apartment unit he owned. Uncle Number Seven introduced us to his sister-in-law, Su Ling, a young woman in a bright orange sundress; and her older brother, Hwa Mang, a husky man flaunting a pearl white polo shirt, navy blue dress slacks, and tasseled leather loafers. Neither spoke English.

After Hoy left to go back to Hong Kong, Number Seven gave us a tour of his sparsely furnished apartment, the highlight being a bathroom with broken tile and pipes piled in the middle of a ruptured bathtub. At least there was a toilet.

My mom informed me that Hwa Mang had invited us all out to eat, but my father shook his head and sat, slump shouldered, by himself, on one of the two torn vinyl-upholstered chairs at the kitchen window. Number Seven tried without success to get my father to change his mind. I didn't know what to make of it. Why would my father want to stay in a hot, stuffy, dilapidated apartment? Was he uncomfortable around my mother and me?

In time our group departed in a van without my father. We traveled a labyrinth of side streets before veering off onto a bumpy dirt road that led to a house. A sign above the door displayed three Chinese characters. To the right of the door a window with diagonal cracks in the pane peered at us like the bloodshot eye of a drunken man.

Our group exited the vehicle and Hwa Mang guided us through a patch of gravel to approach a wooden porch. Aquariums containing live fish, shrimp, and shellfish lined the path and the smell of seawater pervaded. We climbed creaky steps to enter a small and informal restaurant furnished with bare wooden tables and chairs. Two overhead fans whirled with rattling noise. A TV on a counter by the far wall aired a sword fight between mystical Chinese combatants able to backflip over twenty-foot trees. A cash register sat on the end of the counter by a fish bowl of receipts. Behind them a doorway with long dangling string beads. No other customers.

A waiter wearing jeans and a grease-stained T-shirt came

through the beaded curtain to greet Hwa Mang by name. The two joked with each other before the worker directed us to a large round table with a serving wheel at its center. A soaring golden phoenix and a fiery green dragon graced the surface of a gigantic Asian wall fan near us.

We took seats and the man carted out a stack of bowls, teacups, and chopsticks, placing them on the spinning wheel. Next came two metal teapots and a large empty serving bowl. Hwa Mang lit a cigarette, then distributed the dishes and utensils. He lifted a pot and poured tea for the people to his right. Su Ling did the same for our side.

I tapped the table and was about to drink from my cup when my mother said, "Wait."

She dumped her tea into a bowl, dipped her cup's rim into the steaming liquid as if rinsing soap out of it, and did the same to mine. She swirled our chopsticks from both ends in tea and discarded it into the serving bowl.

"What are you doing?"

"Have to wash before eat."

"They don't wash the dishes in China?"

"'Course, but should still clean first."

She didn't offer further explanation, so maybe it was a secondary sanitary measure. Everyone at the table took part in the rinsing ritual. The waiter removed the serving bowl of tea and returned with pencil and pad to take our order. He went through the beaded curtain and came back with more tea, beer bottles for Hwa Mang and Number Seven, and sodas for the kids.

I asked my mom for the children's names.

"The one with big eyes named Chong. The middle boy He Ping. The girl Lin Lin."

Number Seven pushed Chong's head playfully, gestured

in my direction, and the boy smiled. I recalled my mother's annoyance at the fact that Number Seven ignored his daughter at the dinner in Hong Kong with my father.

"Where's Number Seven's wife?"

"They have restaurant in Hong Kong, so she working there, and he come here."

Hwa Mang ordered for us and the waiter brought out small bowls of peanuts. Chong piled a handful into his mouth. He Ping reached for some. Lin Lin didn't move. Su Ling reprimanded Chong and he slipped a couple of peanuts back into his bowl.

Mom spoke to Lin Lin, who was watching everyone else. The girl gave my mother a blank look while placing a peanut in her mouth with all the enthusiasm of a patient opening wide for a drill-wielding dentist.

Number Seven began another of his stories when the waiter appeared with two heaping bowls of spiral-shaped shells.

The "Ahhhs" at our table indicated something delectable.

Hwa Mang exhaled a stream of cigarette smoke and passed out toothpicks. Hands snapped up the shells.

My mom dropped a half dozen in my bowl and they clinked together like marbles.

"What is this?"

"Snails."

"Snails?"

"Is good. Here, I show you." With a shell in one hand and a toothpick in the other, she pried at a small opening until a clump of something squishy emerged. She plopped it in her mouth like an hors d'oeuvre.

I considered myself an open-minded guy. Quyen had no problem getting me to sample Vietnamese dishes. I enjoyed sushi—something she couldn't stomach—made with raw tuna, salmon, and shrimp. But the folks at our table were jabbing into the entrails of garden pests. People poisoned these things to save their plants.

Mom poked the innards of the snail in her hand and dug it out with the end of her toothpick. She gave the stick to me. Holding it aloft, I studied it like something I'd just dissected in Biology lab.

At our table, the others ate heartily. Chong gorged himself on a feast of snails and his brother downed some of his own. Even Lin Lin took part in forcing the slimy creatures from their shells.

Su Ling tapped my arm and motioned for me to eat.

Number Seven said, "Man-Kit," and devoured one to demonstrate.

I brought the snail to my mouth and tried to bite off a tiny piece, but it wouldn't come apart. Holding my breath, I shoved the wad into my mouth and encountered the texture of a rubber band. I chewed at length, swallowed, and gulped some tea.

Number Seven urged me to try another, but I waved my hands. I reached for some peanuts and poured more tea. The smoke from Hwa Mang's cigarette had me wheezing.

Our group made fast work of the snails, and before long, the waiter brought rice and a platter with an entire steamed fish—tail fin, head, gaping mouth, and open eyeball fixing us in its sight—on a bed of dark leafy parsley. A collective "*Wahhhh*" told me this wasn't your garden-variety frozen fish from the local grocery.

Number Seven spooned some of the tender white middle over to Chong.

My mother said, "Wow, this really fresh. I think they just

take from the tank to cook."

Though I liked seafood, there was something disconcerting about eating an animal that had been swimming in an aquarium a half hour ago. I did eat it, but my gaze kept falling on the wax-coated eye, nestled like a jewel on a pillow of parsley, while we carved away its body.

I was relieved at the next plate of Chinese spinach cooked in soy sauce. As the dish went around the table, Hwa Mang signaled to the waiter for another beer by raising his empty bottle. He lit another cigarette. Su Ling said something to him and he gave a terse reply. She stared at him.

Number Seven carried on a monologue. He paused long enough to scoop rice and spinach into his mouth and pull two slips of paper from his shirt pocket.

My mom said, "Chee-se, he showing the grades for the boy again."

I looked at Chong. With bulging eyes behind thick glasses, a flattop haircut, and a long, robotic face on a tree trunk of a neck, he reminded me of Herman Munster. Working on his third bowl of rice, he made Ming look like Morris in front of a bowl of dried cat food.

While the report cards circulated, I asked my mother about Hwa Mang's job.

She interpreted his response. "He manager for the telephone company many years." She added, "I heard that he kind of the playboy. The van from his company, but he need driver come pick us up, because he have accident before. Su Ling tell me he go out drinking and run into another car, so they not let him drive."

This was one of the reasons I had always been so guarded with my mom. Whenever someone confided in me, I considered it a precious gift. I think my mother saw it more like a buffet table, something to be sampled and shared with as many as possible.

The waiter came with a dish of something resembling small, dark, greasy pieces of chicken. Again, an enthusiastic response from our group. Number Seven rubbed his hands together and Chong's eyes swelled even bigger.

I asked my mom what it was.

"That the bird, pigeon."

"Pigeon?"

"Very good, should try."

Chong tore into the pigeon. Number Seven, fingers and mouth dripping grease from ingesting bird flesh, questioned my mother.

"He say how come you not eating?"

"Tell him I'm full. Really full."

* * *

After the feast of slugs, fish eyes, and fowl, we walked back to the van. The sky had dimmed into a burnt orange sunset but it still felt hot as we entered the van.

My mom said, "I think Su Ling's brother use this for business dinner, because he ask for receipt when we go."

"Reimbursement from his work?" I asked.

"Must be. In China, you go higher in company, more power, do less. The company he work must be really taking care of him. You see the way they driving him around? He the really big shot."

She looked at him and scooted closer to me as the vehicle started forward. "At dinner before, his sister talk to him about the beers. I think she really like taking care of people, so she tell him be careful how much he drinking. You know what he say? He say, 'Who the one older, you or me?'"

"So Chinese people mind their elders?"

"'Course. Supposed to be everybody listen to the parents, respect the ones older. Brothers, sisters, too. They live longer, have more experience. You see Su Ling telling Chong not to eat so fast? She like the mother. Good she do that, because he eat more than horse."

I didn't believe in blindly following people just because they had spent more time on this planet, even my parents. My stepfather never pulled a power trip on me, but I always seemed to be in detention with my mother for insubordination. Take high school. I didn't want to march in my graduation. The last thing I needed was to commemorate a lonely and agonizing period of my life. Besides, I didn't think anyone other than my mom would show up.

She insisted on taking pictures at the ceremony and sending them to people I didn't even know. I've never liked myself in pictures and the cap and gown only made it worse. I pleaded with my mother not to send them. She did anyway, so I refused to invite her to my college graduations. To this day Mom hasn't forgiven me.

"Number Seven talking about the boy again. He say Chong going to be successful, make lots money. He never stop about him."

Number Seven had moved forward in the van to regale Hwa Mang and the driver with predictions about Chong's future. Listening, I compared Number Seven's parental expectations with Uncle Chun-Kwok's. They both valued education, but Uncle Chun-Kwok talked about wanting a better life for his children, while Number Seven focused on his son's earning potential, as if the boy were a mutual fund. Chong would be measured by how much money and status he brought to his family. It would be his identity.

I always rebelled against that kind of pressure. What my mother wanted for me, I shunned. Financial security? I chose social services. Marriage? I spent most of my life chasing emotionally frigid women I had zero chance with. Children? I loved kids as long as I didn't have to be responsible for them.

Maybe that's why Quyen's devotion to her family confounded me. At the age of thirty-four she still lived with her parents, Vietnamese immigrants who depended on their children to take care of them in America. Quyen contributed to their income by studying cosmetology and becoming a hairstylist. She cut her family's hair, shopped for their groceries, and rented Vietnamese movies for her parents from their local video store. Quyen helped with the cooking, cleaning, and other household chores. Quyen didn't stay with her parents out of obligation. She enjoyed their companionship and would miss them if she moved out. I couldn't fathom that.

Quyen's dedication to her family made me feel guilty because I didn't help my mom when she opened her restaurant. I rationalized it: my mother made the decision to start a business, so it fell upon her to manage it. I was too busy with work and school to wait tables or wash dishes.

Now I looked at Chong, his face beaming as his father bragged about him. His brother and sister sat silent next to him. The driver let us off at a hotel, and Hwa Mang escorted our group through the double glass doors into an air-conditioned lobby. Chong's tennis shoes squeaked against emerald-green, porcelain tile. The walls boasted dazzling sheets of alternating black and silver mirrored panels, and overhead, a gleaming, triple-layered, beveled-glass chandelier cast a glow upon us.

Hwa Mang went to a shiny black, polished counter and gave instructions to a woman wearing tortoiseshell eyeglasses. She typed into a computer, retrieved a card from below the counter, and handed it to him.

We followed Hwa Mang down an expansive red-carpeted hallway to an elevator. Hotel workers dressed in white greeted him.

My mom scanned the surroundings. "Must be for rich people."

I whispered, "Why are we here?"

She shrugged.

This hotel was unlike anything I had experienced in China. Until now, the people, houses, clothing, and even the restaurants had suggested a simple lifestyle. This place was a study in extravagance, a spot where Donald Trump might vacation.

My mother questioned Hwa Mang. As he responded, her eyes grew wide. She turned to me and said, "Wow, this not hotel! He say this place for vacation, but only people work for his company can use. We stay here tonight."

"These are all employees of the telephone company?"

"The families too. He say have to schedule many months before can use. But he the big shot, so they let us stay. He living here, you know? He have own room."

"Employees get to live here?"

"Only him, because he the manager. Su Ling work for company too, but they give her another place. I'm sure not like this."

We rode the elevator up one floor, where Hwa Mang showed us a nightclub with a parquet dance floor and giant-screen TV. Then he led us into another cocktail lounge, where a hostess whose face was nearly embalmed in pasty white makeup seated our group at two slick, black-upholstered dining booths. Hwa Mang lit a cigarette, drew in a breath, and exhaled a stream of blue. He issued a statement. My mom informed me that we could take part in karaoke.

I said to my mother, "I don't want to be rude, but I'm really tired."

She nodded and relayed the information. Hwa Mang got up, reached into the pocket of his slacks, and handed Su Ling a card. She gestured for me to follow.

My mom said, "She take you go to room."

I stood and thanked Hwa Mang. He dismissed me with a discreet hand motion.

I waved to everyone and went with Su Ling. We took an elevator up another floor and stopped at a door marked with a brass Chinese character. She inserted the card into an electronic slot, and we entered a massive, fully equipped suite with living area, kitchen, and breakfast counter. I saw three bedrooms and two bathrooms.

Su Ling guided me to a spacious room with twin beds separated by a wall counter supporting a reading lamp, digital clock radio, and a remote control unit. The room included a large dresser and huge closet with lacquered wooden hangers.

Su Ling walked to the counter, picked up the remote, and instructed me how to adjust the air-conditioning inside the room. Next she gave me a tour of the kitchen and bathrooms, going so far as to show me the operation of the hot and cold water in the polished brass faucets.

Finally, I said, "*Dak, dak, Dojeh.* You go back to the others and have fun. I'm fine."

She spoke and pointed toward the other bedrooms. My

mother was right about this woman's need to take care of people. I thanked her again and indicated the door.

She smiled, turned, and left.

I went into one of the bathrooms. Like the one at my uncle's house, there was no tub and only a plastic curtain partitioned the shower from the rest of the ivory-tiled floor space. I undressed and took a long shower. As the water funneled into the floor drain, I thought about my father, alone, in Number Seven's small, broken-down apartment.

After showering I brushed my teeth using one of the boxed toothbrushes on the vanity. Even with the floor drain, water had seeped across the tile, so I soaked up the moisture with my towel.

Then I went to my room and set the air conditioner on low. I switched off the lamp and lay on the bed by the window, listening to the low hum of the air conditioner. I didn't go right to sleep. My thoughts drifted back to Quyen. What would she think about this place? Did they have anything like this in Vietnam? And what would she make of my father's decision to remain at Number Seven's apartment instead of accompanying us?

Ghosts 鬼

As my mom and I gathered belongings to leave the resort, I asked her why she thought my father didn't come with us.

"I tell you already. He never like to be with people."

"But he seemed okay with everyone at the dinner in Wan Chai."

"That different, all his family there so he can show off—" She stopped and a kid-who-solved-the-Rubik's Cube excitement appeared in her eyes. "I know, hah! Your father not come because he not have money." Her face shone with a smug satisfaction.

"You mean we're paying to stay here?"

"'Course not. But he prob-ly spend all his money for dinner and gifts for you in Hong Kong. He have to be show off in front of family. That the reason before we never have money. He the big spender even when he not working."

"But you said it's not costing us anything here."

"Not this. If your father go eat with us, he have to be the one pay." She slapped her hands together. "He think he the big shot, buy the expensive dinner and gifts. And he give the money for you go China, too. Must be he broke."

I remained quiet for a moment. "He didn't have to do that."

"You come back to Hong Kong, and he invite his family. He think have to do like that."

* * *

After we thanked Hwa Mang and Su Ling, Number
Seven took my mother and me on the bus to get my father.
Number Seven's children stayed with Su Ling. Throughout
the ride, Number Seven talked, while Mom just stared at
him. I had never seen anyone's verbosity render her silent.

We got off a short distance from Number Seven's
building and walked the rest of the way. At the stairs, I said
to my mom, "Why did we come here yesterday?"

"Maybe Number Seven want to show us apartment
belong to him. Not many people have house in Hong Kong
and apartment in China. He tell me the brother to his wife
live here before."

"What happened to him?"

"He die."

"While living in this building?"

"I not know, but I glad we not stay here. I think the
brother sleep in the bed, the little one in the room?"

I nodded.

"I feel strange to sleep there," she said.

I never imagined my mother to be afraid of ghosts,
but this place did feel strange. The claustrophobic stairs,
the dust-filled apartment almost devoid of furniture, the
crumbling condition of the place—all contributed to a vague
sense of unease.

"Are we going to visit my father's family now?"

"I think so."

"And his parents' graves?"

"That what he say."

* * *

We entered the apartment. My father, wearing the same
clothes as the previous day, greeted us. A man, maybe in his

midthirties, sat on the couch. Sporting a T-shirt that outlined a weightlifter's physique, gym shorts over linebacker-sized thighs, and sneakers without socks, he was a sitting billboard for a health club.

Number Seven broke into conversation with the guy. My father cut in to introduce us to Chai Bo, Number One's son-in-law.

I reached out and prepared myself for a crushing grip. His hand, rough like aged leather, was the opposite of his grasp, which felt light, almost unassuming. He presented a modest smile.

My father retrieved his travel bag from the bedroom and spoke.

Mom said, "We go now. Chai Bo going to drive us."

I went to get our bags, still by the couch where we left them yesterday, and lifted one onto my shoulder. Before I could get the other, Chai Bo took hold of it.

I extended my arm and said, "I can carry it."

He waved his hand and said, "*Dak, dak.*"

I looked to my mother.

"He big, so let him carry," she said.

We followed my father down the stairs and out of the building. Chai Bo deposited our luggage into the trunk of a VW Jetta parked in the alley. He shook Number Seven's hand, and my father also bid good-bye to his brother.

"Number Seven's not coming with us?" I asked.

"He have to get kids and ride bus go back Hong Kong," my mom replied.

She and I thanked Number Seven and climbed into the car.

* * *

The drive on the open road stretched through agricultural fields, cow pastures, fish ponds, and isolated, ramshackle farms. My mother spoke only to Chai Bo, and my father remained quiet. After a little over an hour, we arrived in Chashan, a small town north of Shenzhen. We maneuvered through a maze of twisting turns on narrow paved roads, built more for bicycles than cars. Old two-story, stone houses with sloping, bamboo-ridged roofs lined the path. High cement walls protected many dwellings, and iron bars reinforced windows and entrances.

People loitering near the street watched us drive by. They peered at the car windows, as if they knew we were strangers to this town, foreigners, outsiders.

My mother stayed silent, the way she did at the restaurant when my father first asked us to come here. Chai Bo pulled to a stop by a six-foot-high concrete wall surrounding a towering red-and-gray-brick building. Thick, black wrought-iron bars extended another three feet along the top of the enclosure.

We removed the bags from the trunk, and Chai Bo rang a doorbell at a steel gate. An elderly, stooped woman, wearing the common loose-fitting tunic top and pants, let us in. My mom greeted the woman, who gave a wrinkled-faced smile and nodded at us.

Chai Bo commented, and my mother's expression revealed astonishment. "He say she working here for the family, cook and clean."

We entered a patio containing a koi pond with enormous orange-and-black goldfish. It emitted a pungent, mossy smell.

The house spanned three levels, dwarfing the others in the neighborhood. Balconies protruded from the second and third floors, and iron bars shielded even the highest windows. We took off our shoes at the porch and stepped into a gigantic living area. The sound of a TV could be heard from the other end of the room. A boy, maybe nine, perched with his legs up on a wooden, cushionless couch, watched a cartoon on a twenty-five-inch TV atop a bureau.

The servant brought cloth slippers, and Chai Bo directed us to set our bags by the door. He ushered us into the living quarters. It felt as if we were in a castle—cold bare floors, towering ceilings twenty feet high, and a wide sweeping stone-tiled stairway complete with a polished-wood banister. Situated at the far wing, the steep stairs contributed to an almost medieval air.

I noticed a dining area with an oval, cherry wood table and chairs and a matching china cabinet. An arch entrance led into a spacious kitchen. Compared to the homes in Hong Kong, this seemed like a mansion.

A slender man in a white tank top and forest-green trousers descended the stairs. A statuesque woman with short, straight hair framing a long, narrow face followed him.

The man shook my father's hand and clapped him on the back. The woman spoke her greeting. Then my father introduced them to my mom and me.

My mother said, "His name Mong Soi and she San Fang. He the number one brother and she the wife. He look a lot older than her."

The man must've been in his seventies and the woman in her fifties. I sat between my mother and father on a cushionless cherry wood couch, and Number One and his wife took seats in matching chairs around a hand-carved coffee table.

The servant brought napkins and a large bowl of fresh plums, then served refreshments.

My mother questioned Number One's wife, and the response led to a dialogue. Soon Number One, my father, and Chai Bo joined in. They were discussing the house, but I couldn't make out specifics. I reached for a plum and bit into it. Tart.

In time, more people arrived. A squat, penguin-shaped man came in with a slight, pale-skinned woman in a print dress.

Another man, older, with friendly, engaging eyes helped a physically impaired woman, leaning against him, through the door. The woman's sagging face lacked expression, and her filmy, gray eyes gazed off at an awkward angle.

Chai Bo brought chairs from the dining table, and my mom and I gave our seats to the older man and his companion.

More introductions followed. My mother said, "The man helping his wife, he Kwai Sing, the number two brother. The woman his wife, Li Mei, have stroke three years ago, so he have to taking care for her."

I smiled at them.

"The heavy one Chen-Fang, he number four. The small woman his wife, Gam Lan. They live close by, but Number Two have to come from far away."

It reminded me of the night we met everyone at the restaurant in Wan Chai. I tried to keep it straight. Number One owned the house. Number Two, the helpful one, sat on the couch with his wife who had the stroke. Number Three was overweight. No, that was four. My father was three.

"Number Four not look like the others. He chubby and have more hair."

True. Number One and Two resembled my father. They all shared the same lanky frames, high foreheads, and thin, dark eyes.

The fourth brother seemed to have been birthed from another litter. His paunchier build and wide, loose cheeks gave him the face of a bulldog.

I went to my bag, took out my camera, and said to my mom, "I want to take some pictures of them."

A slight hesitation. She said, "Okay," and spoke to Chai Bo. My mother turned to me and instructed, "Go help him bring more chairs." I handed her my camera.

We positioned a row at the center of the room, and she orchestrated the correct placement of people. She snapped two photos and rearranged individuals.

More shots.

Number One and wife.

Number Two and wife.

Number Four and wife.

All the brothers.

Add me on the end. No, by Number One.

Only the wives.

Everyone together.

Number Two and me.

Switch sides.

Number One's wife and me.

More film.

Number One's wife suggested the servant take a picture of my mom. Then, my mother and me.

My mom hesitated at the third request. My father edged forward. They removed all the chairs except two. My mother cast a wary look at me, at my father, who remained quiet, and all the people in the room.

She stepped slowly toward a chair. My father went to the other. They both scooted to the opposite sides of their seats.

Number One's wife readied the camera, and I realized that for the first time on this trip, my mother and father sat next to each other. Mom leaned forward, rigid, her hands clutching the armrests, eyes bearing straight ahead.

Though my father's face didn't betray his discomfort, I could feel the tension spilling off him, like the scent of fear from a cornered animal.

Number One's wife clicked the shutter. A flash blinded the room. My mother and father didn't move, as if frozen in time. Then my mom stood, the relief on her face replaced by consternation as Number One's wife made another request.

My mother descended slowly onto the chair again.

Number One's wife took the shot. She instructed Chai Bo to place a third chair by my father and signaled for me. She wanted a picture of the three of us, together.

I went to the chair. The tension from the two people beside me became mine. My muscles tightened, heart palpitating. My neck ached, a sharp, jabbing sensation at the base.

Number One's wife snapped the photo, another. And despite the fact that I didn't know whether my legs would hold me, I stood.

As my father got up, I caught a glimpse of my mother. She didn't move. She sat solemn and still, her face blank and lifeless, almost haunted, as if she had taken leave of us and gone somewhere far away.

Education 教育

Chapter 18

Chai Bo's wife, Dai Hin, came home from the sewing machine factory she managed. Dai Hin was Number One's daughter and mother to the boy I saw watching TV. My mom informed me that in China it wasn't unusual to have three generations living under the same roof.

In time the entire group at Number One's house walked to a neighborhood restaurant for dinner. Along the way we passed old, run-down housing. The shelters, crammed together on tiny lots near the road's dirt shoulder, afforded an up-close picture of poverty. No metal gates protected these homes, only drooping, torn chain-link fences. Tattered sheets shielded window frames without glass. A grubby, shirtless, preschool-age boy stood barefoot on the crumbling steps of a falling-apart shack. I hoped he didn't live there, that he had wandered over from another house.

Soon we came to a commercial section of town. Motorcycles and bikes outnumbered automobiles, though none of the riders wore helmets. Young men lounged on parked motorcycles in front of shops and restaurants, smoking and jabbering as if they owned the streets. We encountered rows of chained bicycles blocking the narrow, litter-strewn sidewalk and veered around the loitering motorcyclists. The youths stared at us like hungry wolves eyeing a straggling gazelle.

My mother scooted close and whispered, "We not speak

English outside."

I glanced at the youths again and grasped my mom's reasoning—rich Americans made for crime targets. We entered a restaurant with tables covered in white linen and wooden chairs with peacocks carved into the backs.

A mural spanning the length of one wall paraded a colorful scene of small children, in festive robes of royal red and blue. They chased a plainly dressed peasant boy, who giggled and ran while tugging the string of a kite sailing behind him.

A thin-boned woman, wearing a white blouse and a long black, tapering dress, greeted us.

Number One spoke to her, and she guided us across the restaurant and through a hallway to a separate, private dining area. Wood panels accented the walls, and hexagonal Chinese lanterns with gold dangling tassels hung from the ceiling. A huge round table draped in red cloth took up most of the room.

Our hostess seated me between my father and my mom. Number Two escorted his wife beside my father, helped her onto a chair, and sat beside her. Then came Number One and wife, Number Four and wife, Chai Bo, Dai Hin, and their son.

The hostess departed to be replaced by a fellow wearing a white smock and dark slacks. He brought dishes, chopsticks, a large serving bowl, and two pots of tea.

We rinsed our dishes in tea, and the man removed the tea bowl to return with menus.

Number One ordered for us, and my mom asked what I wanted to drink. I told her water, and she said, "*Seui*," to him.

I said to my mother, "You were really quiet when we were taking pictures. Are you okay?"

"Sure. Why not?"

Her tone discouraged this line of questioning, so I changed the subject. "You warned me not to speak English outside. Did you feel threatened?" I asked.

"Many people poor here. If they know we not from here, maybe they try steal from us. I heard last month, somebody climb the wall the house we stay. They go to top, get in through window, steal the TV. Happen at night, everybody sleep. They make the fence higher after that."

I touched the leather pouch at my waist and checked the back pocket of my jeans for my wallet.

Number One's wife spoke to my mother, and I detected my Chinese name in their conversation. The topic seemed to captivate them because Dai Hin, Number Four's wife, Number One, and even my father chimed in.

Mom broke into an extended discourse. My discomfort grew each time she added more information without translating.

The appearance of our waiter with soup halted them for a moment. Once served, my mother continued where she left off, but I couldn't follow their rapid verbal volleys.

Number Two spooned soup containing small melon chunks into his wife's mouth. I tried mine. Bland.

The waiter brought glasses of brandy for Number One and my father. I tapped my mom's arm. "What were you guys talking about?"

"Oh, they very interested about you and ask about your job." She paused and added, "They also want to know if you get marry soon. So I tell them I not know, because you not tell me about that."

"Great."

"That true. They say you at the age should have wife

and kids. They ask why I not encourage you for that. I tell them the young people different in America. I tell them you stubborn, not like anybody tell you what to do, so not my fault."

I glared at her, and she shrugged.

My father commented and another discussion ensued.

"He say you going out with Vietnam-nese girl. They ask if she speak Chinese."

Not again. I looked at my mother, whose expression lacked any trace of sympathy. Everyone stared at me.

I said, "No," and shook my head.

Silence.

I tried not to slurp my soup and seemed to be the only one eating.

Number Two questioned my mom.

"He want to know more about the girl."

I looked at him and saw a soft reassurance in his eyes.

I began slowly. "Her name's Quyen. We've only been going out a few months, so it's way too early for marriage."

The translation brought a stream of laughter.

Number Two spoke again.

"He want to know what she do."

"She's very close to her family, and she works at a hair salon to help with their income," I said.

After my mom conveyed this, Number Two said something else, and everyone at our table nodded.

My mother reported, "That very important to take care the people you love."

I gazed at Uncle Number Two and the wife he had been spoon-feeding so patiently.

His next comment made my mom light up like a pinball machine.

"He say he heard you have master's degree from college. The Wong family very proud of you. All the Wongs, you the one have the most education."

I regarded him, and he nodded with utter sincerity, the people at our table conferring smiles of agreement.

I looked at my mom, saw my face reflected in her eyes, and I remembered . . . Her hand cupped over mine, our fingers clasping the thick round pencil together. We fashioned the Chinese character in unison on the smudgy newsprint, one after another, again and again, until I could form it on my own.

The sound of her voice, a younger Chinese voice, *"That's right. Good. Now try it again."*

I turned my head, peered up at her. *"Why do I have to keep practicing, Mom?"*

"Keep your concentration."

I continued writing.

"You are so lucky to be able to go to school." She tightened her grip on my hand. *"You must practice, because in this world, people will try to take things from you. But no matter what they do, they can never take what you've learned. Do you understand?"*

Now, I gazed at my mom, down at her hands, the strong, steady fingers that once guided my writing. I studied her and the people at our table.

* * *

That night on the third-floor bedroom of Number One's house, I lay on my twin bed, thinking.

My mother came out of the bathroom in pajamas and sat at the foot of her bed to put on face cream.

Soon, she slipped under her sheets. "Good night, Raymond."

"Good night, Mom."

She switched off the lamp on her nightstand.

In the darkness, I thought about my mother and the memory from my childhood. I said, "Mom?"

"Yes?"

"Did you go to school in China?"

"Little bit. I go school until twelve, then have to run away."

"What about after that?"

"No can do. Have to eat, so I cook, clean houses for people."

"You know all those letters you write to Chinese relatives?"

"Yes."

"How'd you learn how to write like that?"

"When I leave China, I not know if I can see my mother again. Have to learn read, write so can send letters. Otherwise how I can contact for her?"

"Who taught you?"

"Some families I work, they helping me."

We remained quiet. Then, in a hesitant voice, I said, "Did you miss your mother?"

"'Course. But have to be like that."

"How often did you write to her?"

"All the time. Before, I not know if she get the letters. But I keep sending. Later, I know she get because she write back. So I send money for her."

"Money?"

"If I have, I send."

"How'd you know she'd get it?"

"I hope."

I pictured my mom as a child learning to read and write,

cooking and cleaning for families to send money to her mother. I thought about my father and how he wanted me to meet his family. My family.

My mother's translation echoed in my mind. *"The Wong family very proud of you. All the Wongs, you the one have the most education."*

Mom had told me about Uncle Number Two and his wife, the great distance from their home to Chashan, the hardship of riding the bus due to her condition. They couldn't attend many of the recent family gatherings.

Yet they were here now. I didn't know what to think. All my life, the term "family" had held no real meaning.

Now I was discovering people and relationships I couldn't have imagined. And I had a feeling this was just the beginning.

Ancestors 祖先

Chapter 19

Thick black clouds masked the early morning sky and heavy rains blanketed Chashan. Number One pulled a jeep up to the front gate. Number Two, my father, my mom, and I met him outside. The others climbed into the old and rusty four-seater, which featured a canvas top extending over a small cargo hold. I sat on a step stool in the cramped tail section next to the spare tire and an empty gas can. The smell of gas and oil overwhelmed my senses.

We drove to Number Four's house. The ride was bumpy, jarring at times. Though enclosed, the very back of the hold remained exposed, like a tent with a flap missing, and rain puddled onto its metal deck. The tight, two-lane road cut through vast stretches of soggy crop fields. Again the disparity between the amount of land in Hong Kong and China struck me. It felt like going from a dinky studio apartment in a crowded tenement to a rugged, old-style ranch house.

After a while, we came to a neighborhood of mundane, gray stone houses. I peeked out to see us stop at a modest, one-story home with a rain-soaked cement walk leading to a covered porch. Number One honked his horn, which hacked out the sound of a trombone after it had been dropped down three flights of stairs. Moments later Number Four broke from the house. Scrunching under an umbrella, he held two batches of flowers encased in clear plastic. He slogged toward us, talked briefly with Number One, and scooted around to the rear.

He set his flowers on the deck, closed and tossed the umbrella in the hold and, showing surprising agility, hoisted his wide girth into the compartment. I got up and offered him the stool. He shook his head, but I insisted. He regarded me, nodded, picked up his flowers, and sat.

The jeep lurched and I nearly tumbled. Number Four grabbed my arm, and after regaining my balance, I sat on the lip of the spare tire. The drive reminded me of an off-roading excursion, as time and again our vehicle collided with one of the numerous potholes. The deck was sopping as water swirled in from the opening. It didn't help that our cubbyhole rendered the disorienting sensation of seeing objects shrink from us.

We veered onto an isolated muddy road and drove up an incline to a rough stretch of barren earth and surrounding red-clay hillsides. Number One drew to a stop on level terrain and shut off the engine. We sat in a downpour, swamped in mud and rocks.

No one spoke, so I waited. It must've been twenty minutes before the rain let up. I heard the jeep doors creak and the sound of Number One's voice. My mother and father soon appeared with Number One and Two. Number Four hitched himself out of our hold, plopping into the muck, and I did the same. He retrieved the flowers.

Number One guided us in a chilly, light rain toward a muddy, craggy red hill about a hundred feet from our vehicle. Number Four left his umbrella in the jeep, and none of the others brought one. Behind my father I noticed beads of moisture in the filmy strands of his hair. His black patent-leather shoes sunk into grimy orange-red goop with each stride.

When we arrived at the base of the hill, Number One gave a directive and headed up while Number Four, still holding the flowers, helped Number Two. I started up, turned, and extended a hand to my mom. My father followed us.

With no trail in sight Number One improvised his own. Though the slope wasn't steep the wetness made for treacherous footing. I climbed slowly, trying to anchor my tennis shoes with each step. I held my mother's hand and instructed her to put her feet where mine had been. At one point, the moist clay slid out from under me and I had to plant my knee into a glob of soil.

She said, "Chee-se, you okay?"

I nodded and patted the sludge from my pants. "Be careful, it's slippery in this spot."

Mom relayed the message to my father and we moved ahead. Finally we reached the top of a bluff that provided a panoramic sweep of an expansive valley. A thick nest of trees lined the horizon beyond.

Further along the bluff, a row of four-foot-high cement slabs emerged. Spaced in neat rows, they seemed to gaze out at the valley. Our group gathered at the largest of them, which resembled a miniature shrine. It included a stone arched roof supported by four concrete pillars and a cement foundation that brought to mind something out of ancient Greece.

A polished granite headstone showed two black-and-white pictures of an elderly man and woman and eight embedded Chinese characters beneath. Three stone urns rested at the foot of the shrine, a rectangular one between two smaller, vase-shaped twins.

Number One took out several sticks of incense from his jacket. He stuck one into the ashes of the urns and lit each with a cigarette lighter. Wispy lines of smoke and the smell of sage infused the air.

Number One knelt in front of the pictures, the knees of his pants soaking in the moisture on the cement. He put his hands together in prayer and closed his eyes. In a few moments he stood and Number Two assumed his position. Then my father. Number Four passed the flowers to him and followed their example.

My father came up, handed me one batch of flowers, and spoke.

I looked at my mom.

"This the place they bury the mother and father," she said. "He die many years ago. She die last year. He want you put flowers for them, and he ask you pray too."

"I'm not sure I know how."

"You see the way they do? You follow them."

My father indicated to me, and I stepped forward. He pointed to the flowers and to the rectangular urn.

"You want me to put them there?"

He nodded.

I set them next to it and he motioned me downward with his hand. I knelt on the cement and gazed at the picture of the two people. The woman's thin, angular face bore a resemblance to my father and his older brothers. Her hair, cropped short, revealed a high, rounded forehead. The man, his face fuller, observed me with dark, riveting eyes. Number Four looked like him.

That's when it struck me. These were my grandparents. I never knew my mom's parents. She had not spoken of them to me until we came to Hong Kong. My stepfather's family was every bit as much a mystery. Once, I asked about them for a school assignment. His response, *"I'm from Minnesota. Just leave it at that."*

Now I stared at the pictures of my grandparents. Who were they? Where had they lived? Had they been close to my father? Had they known about me?

The cold, daunting realization set in that I would never be able to ask them, and I felt a heaviness in my chest, a sadness for two people I had never even met.

I put my hands together, closed my eyes, and prayed in silence. A calm came over me, a deep, overriding serenity at the core of my being. In time I opened my eyes, studied the faces of my grandparents, locking each in my mind. I stood before the shrine, a memorial to my grandparents. Though I wasn't a religious man and wouldn't have been able to define the ritual I had just performed, I understood the importance. I felt it.

Number One led our group to a smaller headstone next to my grandparents'. This one revealed an image of a man with thick eyebrows and the now familiar receding hairline. We all prayed again and I placed the second set of flowers at this shrine. Then we walked to the edge of the bluff and gazed out at the valley.

My mom came to me and said, "This grave the one for brother number five. He die last year."

I nodded.

"They tell me on the way here the mother die last year not long after him. She really upset about him."

"What about the father?"

"He die many years ago. Number Seven tell me before they not have good place for bury him. The ground flat and not high, so no view. He say bad luck for family because that. His business not good, brother and mother die. So the brothers give money, move the graves here. This open, high, good view for them."

"For the visitors?"

"No, for the mother, father, Number Five. They need good place for how you say, ghosts . . . ?"

"Spirits?"

"Maybe that. Spirits need good place to rest. He say they move the graves here, and luck change for the family. Everybody healthy, and you come back to Hong Kong."

I regarded her. "My coming here was important to them?"

"You the only son for your father."

I reflected on this. "Why is the location of the grave so important?"

"Have to respect the parents, even when they die. If put them in bad place, they unhappy, bring bad luck to family. Number Seven say should visit the grave every year. One year, he very busy, so he not visit. He say he never do again because his business bad that year."

I said, "If he's going to visit, it should be to pay his respects, not for his business."

She nodded. "That how should be."

My father conveyed something to my mom.

She said, "We go now."

The descent was more of an adventure. While climbing, I could at least push off from a foothold. Heading down I took my chances on where I planted my feet on the unstable rock and clay. The rain grew heavier.

Again Number Four assisted Number Two. My mother held my arm. With sneakers on her small feet, she fared better than my father, whose slick-soled leather shoes must've made for footing comparable to sledding on a bed of marbles.

I couldn't help them both, so I hoped he would be okay. When my mom and I reached safe ground, my father labored twenty feet behind. I went up to assist, but he shook his head and shooed me away. Red clay caked his shoes and pant legs, and moisture soaked his print shirt. Still he managed, and once on the bottom, he slapped his hands together as if he had just finished a leisurely stroll in the park. His clothes appeared more as if he had been mauled by a mountain lion. He brushed his hands against his slacks, which did nothing to lessen the impression.

We trudged to the jeep and drove out of the cemetery amidst a pouring rain.

Commitment 承諾

Chapter 20

On the way back from the cemetery, I thought about
my grandparents' shrine, their solemn faces in the pictures
on the headstone, and the feeling of peace that pervaded
as I prayed before them. I didn't know what to make of it.
For a moment, I was connected to something beyond me,
something incomprehensible. Two weeks ago, I would've
scoffed at the idea of paying homage to the ghosts of
deceased ancestors. Now, it seemed anything but far-fetched.

I thought of Quyen. She invited me once to a Buddhist
temple for Tet, the Vietnamese equivalent to Chinese New
Year. Vibrant yellow flowers in fine porcelain vases, exotic
food offerings, and the fragrance of burning incense
filled the colorful, ceremonial worship room. In front of
an elaborate stage decorated by glistening urns of every
size and shape, she knelt in tribute to a towering, bronzed
Buddha.

She told me later she had prayed for her parents' health
and well-being. Without an inkling of self-consciousness, she
added that she did the same every night before going to bed.
Quyen said if she kept her parents in her heart and prayers,
Buddha would bless and safeguard them.

At the time, I thought it peculiar to hold one's parents
on such a pedestal. Now, with everything I had experienced
the past week and a half, the bond forged with my uncle's
family, my father, his relatives—mine, it didn't seem so

strange.

I wanted to share these discoveries. I wanted to call Quyen.

We dropped Number Four off and drove to Number One's house in a downpour. We appeared to be the only vehicle brave or foolhardy enough to venture out in these conditions.

Number One stopped at his gate and we all got out. On the porch, my father, hands sweeping mud from his clothes, spoke to me.

My mother translated, "He ask if you comfor-ble to see the graves."

I turned to him. "Yes. It was an experience I'll never forget."

She studied me a moment, then relayed it.

We went into the house and he said something else. My mom's tone was subdued. "He say you can always come here visit, anytime is okay."

I looked at him and said, "*Dojeh.*"

*   *   *

After going upstairs to change, I came back to the living room, soon to be joined by my mother, Number Two, and his wife. My father, holding a thick, letter-sized envelope, descended the stairs alongside Number One.

My father went over to my mom, and as they talked, she kept glancing at me. He presented her the envelope. She opened it, glimpsed the contents, and engaged in more discussion. She attempted to return it, but he refused, pointing to me.

She said to me, "They know we going to Peking, so they want give us money for trip."

"He's already given us money."

My father spoke. Mom said, "He want make sure we not run out. He say better have too much than not enough."

"He doesn't have enough to give us, and we don't need it."

My father, hands upraised, issued a staunch declaration.

"He say he your father, and he want you take."

I looked at my mother.

"He insist about that."

I remembered her words at Uncle Chun-Kwok's house the night before we departed for China, "—*you too much concerned. . . . They let you stay, take care of you because you the family. That how Chinese people do.*" I nodded to my father and said, "*Dojeh,*" in a quiet voice.

He smiled.

My mom said, "Number One give, too."

I said to Number One, "*Dojeh,* Daaihbaak."

My use of the term signifying his status as my senior uncle brought appreciative laughter from him. He and my father spoke at the same time.

"They say you doing good, keep practicing the Chinese."

* * *

While my mother rested upstairs, I stood at the window in the living room watching the rain.

"Man-Kit." The sound of my Chinese name, so unfamiliar until this trip, snapped me out of my thoughts. Number Two, sitting with his wife on the cushionless teakwood couch, motioned for me. I walked up to him and he reached out as if to lead a child across an intersection. I extended my hand and he grasped it like a fragile keepsake before putting my hand in his wife's wobbling, fleshy palm.

All the while, he talked in a gentle, rhythmic voice, as if I could comprehend his words.

I knelt by his wife. Though her gray, glassy eyes gazed off, I could feel her presence. Her fingers, shaking, clasped mine in a delicate embrace, her mouth opening a bit as if to smile. Spittle ran down the corner and her husband took out a handkerchief to dab her cheek and chin.

I held her hand as her husband spoke in a solemn, steady cadence. I listened as if he was my best friend imparting guidance before my wedding. I saw warmth in his eyes and an acceptance achieved through struggle and sacrifice.

He spoke in a manner that told me he was baring his soul, and I felt honored to share in his story. I didn't know how long we remained like this but I wanted to hear every word.

When he finished he peered at me, studying my face as if to inscribe this precious moment in posterity. He gave a gracious smile and I knew we had exchanged something profound. I felt I had known him my entire life. This was a reunion rather than a meeting and I thought of how lucky I was to take part in it.

I regarded him, my uncle, my father's older brother, a man who shared a world with the woman he adored. I also saw pain in his eyes, the kind which could only stem from bearing the suffering of the most important person in his life, of being completely powerless to change it. But in spite of that, his eyes, soft brown and welling with truth, told me he would do it all again without a second thought. He would walk with his wife, feed her, nurse her until her last dying breath. Or his. Of that I was certain.

I looked at my uncle, then his wife. And the idea of marriage didn't seem so scary.

Wounds 傷口

Chapter 21

The sound of a car horn outside signaled my mother
and me. She rose from the couch, approached Number One,
and took his hand in both of hers to exchange good-byes.
She did this with his wife, Number Two, and his spouse. And
though she didn't extend her arms to my father, she thanked
him.

I went to each relative and copied my mom's method
of conveying farewell. When I came to Uncle Number Two,
I grasped his hands for a long moment and said, "*Dojeh,
Yihbaak.* Thank you for coming."

He smiled at my reference to him as the second eldest
uncle. He placed a palm on my shoulder and spoke my
name in a tone of friendship. I moved to his wife and
clasped her hand. An almost imperceptible movement of her
mouth told me she was pleased.

I stepped up to my father, gripped his hand, and our
eyes met. There was so much I wanted to say. He peered at
me and gave a nod of understanding.

Then my mother and I walked to the car.

* * *

Dark, ominous skies threatened rain as Chai Bo drove
us on a small, two-lane highway to visit my mom's friend in
Guangzhou. We passed fields of rice, cabbage, and tea.

In the front seat my mother watched a group of peasants
wearing wide-brimmed straw hats, bending to pick tea leaves

from the shrubs, and putting them into wicker baskets.

"Chee-se, see how hard they working here?"

She said it as if trying to convince me of the rigorous life in China, that Hwa Mang's resort and Number One's spacious home were anomalies.

I said, "How did Number One get such a nice house?"

"He working in some kind factory before. Government give land, and he build. Dai Hin very successful, so I think she helping him with money."

"That's a pretty generous daughter."

"That how Chinese people do. She and Chai Bo living there, so help them too. I heard all the brothers give money for Number One build the house, except your father."

"What do you mean?"

"He the only one not give."

"Who told you that?"

"Number Seven say so. He talking a lot about the house. He say all the brothers agree to help Number One, but your father selfish because he not want to give. I think he prob-ly just not have money."

"He had enough to give us for Beijing."

"He get from Number One." She said it with the unabashed certainty of a woman who had been with my father long enough to know.

* * *

We rode in silence observing water buffalo–drawn plows carve lanes into open fields while laborers, squatting in ankle-deep ponds, strung together rice stalks to plant in the muddy water.

My mother started a conversation with Chai Bo. In time she turned to me and said, "He working for his wife's business. They making all kinds clothes and shipping to Hong Kong, too."

"Good."

She lowered her voice. "I heard that they meet at work, but she higher than him. Dai Hin the same like me, she work hard, move up in company. She own now."

"Sure."

"For some people, can be problem for wife to have higher position than husband, but he not upset about that."

"Yeah."

"Something wrong with you?"

I leaned forward to face her. "Did my father ever have a problem with you working?"

She shot me an incredulous look. "Chee-se, if not for me, we not have enough eat, I tell you that. Sometimes, he working few hours, sometimes nothing. A family must be have money for food and rent."

"He seems to be supporting himself now."

"That little place he living? No furniture, no car, nothing? He always poor. Never change."

"Maybe that's how he wants to live."

Her voice grew louder. "Who want that? Just one room, have to share the house with other people, everybody use the kitchen, prob-ly have to wait in line to cook. You want that?"

"We've been in the US. Things are different there."

"You see Uncle Chun-Kwok? He come to Hong Kong after your father, but he have house, two houses. He have good job, stable, taking care his family. Even Number Seven have house in Hong Kong and apartment in China. He not just fooling around, do nothing, have nothing, and spend go all his money on gifts for son he not care about."

For a moment the words didn't register, my mind unable

to comprehend what she had just mouthed. Then the impact hit with the full force of a hand grenade. My entire body went numb.

Shock appeared in my mother's eyes. She turned from me, like a soldier who couldn't bear to face the remains of an enemy she had just blown up.

Her words reverberated in my mind. Over and over. My heart pounded, muscles tightened. The dark feeling surged in me again. The same black, searing anger that engulfed me at Victoria Peak when the woman berated Jing-Wei.

Before I could contain it, the venom spewed out. "At least he gave me something, which is more than Roger ever did."

"No."

"It's true and you know it. Roger never wanted me around and that's how he treated me."

"He do like that because he drinking too much."

"He didn't drink too much to go to Michael's football games. He was never too drunk for that."

"What you want me do, get divorce? Okay, we citizens now, not need you. That what you want?"

Our eyes locked, but neither of us spoke. My heart was slamming the inside of my chest, my mind spinning out of control. I stared at this woman: craning to watch me, brow furrowed, deep lines knifing across her forehead. She waited for my response.

I knew what my mother anticipated, the answer she was bracing for. And I wanted to say it, to make her taste the kind of pain I had known throughout my childhood.

Only now as I peered at my mother, some force—a gigantic, benevolent hand—reached down and held me back. I stopped, slowly shook my head, and turned to the empty fields. I tried to breathe. The air would not enter my lungs.

My face, my entire body felt hot, as if I had been running blindly, going nowhere.

Then it struck, raw and naked. First in my face, then sinking down into my chest and stomach. Shame.

I had seen my mother and stepfather fight with the viciousness of rabid animals and vowed I would never do that. Now there was more than a part of me that wanted to destroy another human being—my own mother.

Neither of us spoke for a long time. Chai Bo, nervous eyes darting at me through the rearview, drove us down the desolate road.

My mom broke the silence. "Raymond, I not mean what I say about your father."

I didn't respond.

"Raymond."

"Maybe you're right about him."

"No, that not true. He not good with money, but he care about you a lot. He so happy you come back to Hong Kong, he invite all the family to see you."

I nodded.

"Roger, he close to Michael, that true, but he not try hurt you."

"It doesn't really matter."

"When we get marry, he tell me he taking care for you, just like his own son. He try, but hard for him to do."

"He never really tried."

"He do, but he not know how."

I studied my mom, her earnest expression.

She continued, "That true. I heard that he not close to his family, so maybe not easy for him care about son not belong to him."

I gazed out at the deserted highway. Roger and I had

never been close throughout my childhood. In his mind, I watched TV too much. I was dumb, "*D-U-M-B*," because I didn't pay attention. I couldn't fix things with my hands. I was always reading. I never helped around the house. I was shy and withdrawn. There was something really wrong with me.

So I pulled away from him and built a wall I never lowered. Then when Michael was born, I saw the difference. Roger's eyes showed a man looking at his own son.

My mother said, "I know Roger alone a lot. Michael go away to school. Renee not get along with him. I have business. He the only one at home. He lose job, so nothing for him do. I tell him go find another job, but . . ."

My mom's words trailed off. We passed a lone cargo truck carrying a wooden bed full of sheep. The planks of the hold formed thick bars trapping the animals inside.

"What do you think will happen to him?" I said.

A disquieting contemplation appeared on her face. "Maybe he find something to do. Maybe somebody helping him." Her words rang with the hollowness of a person who didn't believe herself.

"Mom, that's what you've been doing since you married him. I don't think there's any more you can do."

"He still drinking."

"You're not responsible for that."

"But—"

"You can't make him stop."

She looked at me with the eyes of a woman unwilling to give up. "I work so hard, try to do right thing. But he just drinking, drinking all the money gone. Why he cannot see that?"

I didn't say anything.

"Why he do that?"

"Maybe that's all he has."

She stayed silent. Then in a voice filled with sorrow, she said, "He has me."

Hardship 艱困

Chapter 22

Chai Bo drove my mom and me to a tenement in Guangzhou, a sprawling city in southern China that my mother still referred to as Canton, the name used prior to the Chinese Communist Revolution. We met my mom's childhood friend, Wai Fong, at her house. The woman's whole appearance came out in geometric angles, from the sharp corners of her trapezoid-shaped eyeglasses to her short, puffy triangular hairstyle and the small, narrow points of her elbows and shoulders. Even her movements seemed disjointed, as if her anatomy was somehow misaligned.

Wai Fong introduced us to her family: her husband, Sung Bok, a man who saw it as his life's mission to put more pounds on my skinny frame by feeding me nonstop; their son, Cheun Chi, a quiet person with a keen interest in military history; and his wife, Mei Heng, a young lady whose brusque demeanor toward me suggested a slab-sized chip on her shoulder. Mei Heng was the only one who spoke English.

We shared spirited conversation and a home-cooked meal of sautéed string beans with garlic, an entire fish bathed in a deep-fried batter, and a plate of shrimp and cabbage. My mother and Wai Fong reminisced into the evening. Then Cheun Chi and Mei Heng insisted we sleep in their nearby apartment because it provided more comfort, and they offered to stay with Wai Fong for the duration of our visit.

Wai Fong and her son led my mom and me into an alley to walk to his place. Torn-up potholes impeded our path, and dark, faceless walls pinned us in on either side. The lingering stench of something dank and decaying overpowered my senses in the stillness of the night.

I shouldered a travel bag and walked behind Wai Fong, who guided us with a flashlight. She held on to my mother's arm, as if leading a child across a treacherous intersection. Cheun Chi, toting my mom's bag, flanked them to the right. The flashlight's narrow beam penetrated the darkness, allowing us to avoid piled boxes of garbage or empty crates strewn about. I said, "How far is this place?"

"Wai Fong tell me it close by. You remember she say her son and Mei Heng come visit all the time?"

"Right." A moment later I asked, "What does Mei Heng do?"

"Some kind import business, so her English helping her for that." She lowered her voice. "I heard her husband go out lots girls before, some very pretty. He picky, so not want to marry." She fired a glare at me. "She skinny, really not pretty, but she the one he choose. Maybe that the good way."

"For who?"

"That working for them."

A strained silence. I broke it. "Did she seem friendly to you?"

"Sure. She tell me a lot. Why you ask?"

Mei Heng made a number of comments to me about the US culture that bordered on rudeness—remarks about the superficial and extravagant excesses of our cars and clothes, as if America somehow grated on her. I wondered if I had unknowingly insulted her in some way. "It's probably nothing."

Wai Fong's "close by" stretched a lot farther than my
definition. We turned corner after corner, weaving around
alley potholes to a lone beam of light that exposed gigantic
cockroaches scurrying along the ground. The size of small
rodents, they could've starred in a Stephen King movie. It
made me thankful we walked in the dark, because God only
knew how many of them infested the alley. Wai Fong talked
to my mother in a tone one might use strolling through
Balboa Park on a hazy Sunday afternoon.

Finally, we stopped at steps in front of an eerie stone
building, where darkness partially concealed towering
double doors. My imagination went to work on what awaited
us inside.

Wai Fong climbed the steps and aimed the light at the
keyhole. Her son unlocked the door, shoved it hard, and
it swung back with a loud, rickety sound. We entered an
enclosed, shadowy space and needed to duck under a line
of clothing. Down a tight hallway, I heard televisions inside
rooms. Empty plastic pails hung on the opposite wall, and
buckets of clothes soaking in water created another obstacle
in our path.

Near the end of the hall, Cheun Chi opened a door and
flicked a light switch. We stepped into a dinky studio smaller
than the living room of my San Diego apartment. A tiny
couch with stubby metal legs and thin vinyl cushions took
up most of the room. Its advantage must've been portability
because it didn't look the least bit comfortable.

The place brought to mind the scrunched conditions in
Hong Kong: up against the couch, an old refrigerator with
a toaster oven on top; square aluminum table in a corner
and metal folding chairs stacked underneath; near the
door, a TV braced on a board between cement blocks; large

white Thermos next to a tray of glasses and dishes by the TV; wooden ladder attached to the wall in another corner, probably leading to an attic or storage area.

Cheun Chi and I dropped our bags by the couch on the cold, hard cement. Wai Fong took my mom and me to the refrigerator, opened it, and pointed to a plastic pitcher on a shelf. Apart from that and a few condiment jars, the refrigerator was empty. She directed my mother to the Thermos and gave instructions while flipping the top open to allow a trail of vapor to escape.

Mom said to me, "This the hot water. If we need for wash or drink, can use."

"Drink?"

"She say have to boil water to drink. The one in 'frigerator okay, already boiled, but if need more, use from here."

"What do you mean if we need to wash?"

"The bathroom outside."

Wai Fong went outside to bring back a bucket. She placed it under the Thermos and depressed a lever to release steaming water. She shut it off and handed the bucket to her son. Wai Fong retrieved plastic grocery bags from under the couch, then headed out into the hallway. Cheun Chi carried the bucket after her, and my mother and I followed.

Wai Fong lifted a Tupperware bowl from a rusty nail on the wall and walked to the end of the corridor. She opened a moldy wooden door to reveal a dimly lit space that approximated the area of a custodial closet. I saw a dirty sink, with an equally grimy rubber hose attached to a faucet. Pails of various sizes lay scattered on a counter blackened by sludgy filth, and the cement floor reminded me of my high school auto shop.

Wai Fong spread the plastic bags on the counter. Cheun Chi set the bucket on them and directed the nozzle to fill the container. Wai Fong scooped water out with the Tupperware bowl and slowly poured it into the sink while explaining to my mom.

My mother said, "Only cold water from here, so have to bring hot water to make warm for take a shower."

"Shower?"

"She say use the soap to wash and bowl for rinse off. Take plastic bags to put clothes and towel. Put more bags on ground to step on so feet not get dirty."

"We bathe here?"

"Not only us. Everybody in building."

"A communal shower?"

"That what she say, so have to make sure lock the door."

On cue, Wai Fong shut the door and fastened the steel hook to trap us in.

My mom said, "They wash dishes here too."

I once visited a board-and-care facility for mentally ill patients in San Diego and thought the accommodations inadequate and demeaning. Compared to this, that was the Waldorf-Astoria.

Wai Fong unclasped the hook. Cheun Chi emptied the bucket and gathered the plastic bags. We followed his mother out. She stopped at the only door on the other side of the hall and forced it open. Wai Fong pulled a string chain and an outhouse appeared complete with a cement floor basin and a wretched smell.

"Let me guess, the toilet."

Mom didn't respond.

Wai Fong, with Tupperware bowl, simulated dumping water into the hole.

My mother said, "After use, put water."

Was this why Mei Heng had reacted so strongly at my mere mention of the American lifestyle? Did she see me as a rich and pampered brat? Could that be why she didn't accompany us here?

* * *

Back at the studio, I said to my mom, "Her son lives here?"

"Maybe they just sleeping here at night. Prob-ly they spend most the time at her house."

To think they actually brought us here to make us more comfortable! Wai Fong spoke to my mother and indicated the ladder in the corner.

My mom said, "Another room up there. She say one sleep on couch, and one sleep up there."

"A room?"

"Go see." She said something to Cheun Chi, who hand-beckoned me to climb up after him.

At the top he flipped a light switch on the wall. He stepped off the ladder and crouched to avoid the low ceiling, and I followed him to a tiny loft with a mattress, lamp, clock radio, and electric fan on the ground. Four feet separated the ceiling from the floor. On the ceiling above the mattress, a poster displayed a shirtless Chinese man in jeans embracing an equally barebacked young woman in his arms. They could've been Asian models for Calvin Klein.

I pointed to it, and Cheun Chi shrugged as his face became flushed. He knelt to show me how to turn on the fan and lamp, then led me down the ladder.

In the studio, Wai Fong spoke to my mother and gestured to the TV and refrigerator.

Mom said, "*Dak, dak.*"

Wai Fong persisted, and my mother practically dragged her by the arm to the door. Cheun Chi escorted his mom out, and moments later, I heard Wai Fong call to us from down the hall.

My mother shouted, "*Dak, dak, dak,*" and bolted the three locks and the chain on the door. She went to the couch, swiped her hands together, and plopped down as if we had just checked into a hotel.

Standing in the middle of the room, I said, "What do you think about this place?"

My mom shook her head. "Boy, I really glad I not living in China."

I stared at her. "This is horrible!"

Her expression grew serious. "Before when I run away from my hometown, I living worse than this."

"Really?"

"Sure. Sometimes no have place sleep. This nothing. If I stay China, maybe my house like this."

I tried to picture it. Couldn't. It just wasn't my mother.

I went to my travel bag and took out a T-shirt and sweats. "I can't believe this. That bathroom. People bathe in there!"

"You used to America, but before in Hong Kong, we stay the place smaller than Uncle Chun-Kwok's. We sharing with two other families."

"Did we have a room?"

"We sleep in living room, mattress and blankets on the floor. We have crib for you in corner."

An image, a trace of a time long past, surfaced in my mind: a tiny, crowded space, an open window, drapes, the smell of sewage, people talking outside, yelling nearby—close, another room, a man and a woman, a baby crying. . . .

The memory, drifting and tenuous, slipped away. I shook my head.

"That why I take you go from Hong Kong. If we stay, maybe always bad, maybe you not have education. You grow up, I not know what you do."

I sat on the couch beside my mom. "If you had remained in Hong Kong, what do you think you'd be doing?"

She paused, a blank look on her face. "I used to working cleaning hotels. Maybe that, maybe waitressing. No can tell."

"Didn't you own a house before?"

She flashed a proud smile. "Not many women do that."

"What happened to it?"

"I buy to use for family, but when that man attacking me, I know no can stay Hong Kong." My mother pressed her fingers to her temples as if to induce the sequence of events from her memory. "Uncle Number Five also run from China before. In Hong Kong, he have wife and little boy. When I buy house, his family move in with me, your father, and my sister, Daaihyih. After we leave Hong Kong, your father move out. Then, Uncle Chun-Kwok write to America, tell me he need place stay in Hong Kong, so I say he can use my house."

"So Uncle Chun-Kwok lived with Number Five and his family?" I recalled Number Five's picture on the headstone in Chashan. Of my uncles, Mom spoke about him the least.

"Daaihyih living there too, but after we go, she die from stroke. Then you know what Number Five do?" A profound disgust appeared on my mother's face, and she slapped her hands together as if striking at an annoying fly. "He tell me he helping me out, want to pay the property tax. I think he really nice do that, but later"—she shook her head—"he hire lawyer say the house should belong to him because that!"

She scooted closer and emphasized the extent of his

betrayal by jabbing her index finger at me as she spoke.

I suddenly feared for the safety of my eyes.

"He tried to take the house?"

"You believe that? Really he no good. I hire the lawyer, very expensive, go fight in court. They send me the papers, I call the lawyer, talk, send more money, lousy."

"You processed the whole case from the US?"

"I decide go back to Hong Kong, too much trouble take care everything from America. Number Five really no good. He know I take long trip, so try to go slow, waste time. My lawyer tell me should sell house for him, get some money, not so much headache."

"You didn't sell it to him, did you?"

"Number Five think should be his! But my lawyer talking his lawyer. They both say he should buy."

"You agreed?"

"I really not want that, but my lawyer say that the good thing. If I fight more, cost lots money, not sure who win. So I sell house for him, get rid that, go home."

"Did you at least come out ahead?"

"If not for him I sell for more."

"What'd you do with the money?"

"Use some to help buy house in America. Daaihyih die by then, so I send money for her son."

It was an understatement to say my mother knew how to handle finances. She had borrowed money from her sister to invest in Hong Kong real estate when most women were content to be housewives. It wasn't luck because she also purchased property in the US. No doubt that without her scrimping and management of our family's income, we would never have been able to afford a house in San Diego. And my brother, Michael, would not have been attending

USC.

Now I was experiencing a different side of my mom,
a woman who bought a house in Hong Kong and then
returned the proceeds from the property's sale to her
nephew after her sister's passing.

I reflected on this in silence. Thoughts of Uncle Number
Five's betrayal seeped into my mind. "It doesn't make sense
that Number Five would try to scam you," I said.

"The house worth money, so he want for himself."

"If he lost in court he would've been out on the street."

My mother sat up on the couch and leaned toward me.
"You not understand, because you always have enough eat,
bed to sleep. But in China, different. I cook, clean, borrow
the money from friends. Sometimes, still not enough." Her
eyes looked straight into mine. "Sometimes I have to go to
market. The seller busy, not watching, I take some bread,
vegetables, run fast. Sometimes I go to garbage behind
restaurant, dig for something can eat."

Her voice was measured, steady, without a hint of
remorse, and I knew she would do it again if she needed to.

She said, "That the way when you no have money."

"Was that why you left my father?"

Her eyes popped open, as if the question caught her by
surprise. Her momentary disorientation transformed into
a steely glare. "If I stay with your father, we have nothing,
always poor. I know about that kind life."

Her expression told me she knew all too well.

"Do you think you did the right thing?"

"Right, wrong, who know? For me, very hard to leave.
I know it hurt your father. You the only son. I take you go,
he have nothing. But if I stay, you grow up Hong Kong do
what? Maybe you not have chance for education. Education

very important, you know. Nobody in my family have chance for that before . . ."

For one of the few times in my life, I detected a note of regret in my mom's words.

"Do you wish you could've gone to school?"

"What good think about that now? For me, no choice."

A long silence. When she spoke, her voice was subdued. "I thinking a lot. I see Wai Fong, how she living with her family, how people living in Hong Kong, Uncle Chun-Kwok, Poi Yee, your father . . ." Though she gazed at me, she seemed to be speaking to herself. "Maybe one time that kind life okay for me. But when Communists take my hometown, what they do to my mother, father . . . I no can stay. Have to go. Have to go."

Her words, barely audible, induced a disquieting feeling of eavesdropping on a private conversation.

She sat motionless for long minutes, staring past me. Slowly, her eyes refocused and she came back. "I need tell you. Before this trip, I plan to ask you something. But maybe you think it strange, so I wait. In Hong Kong, I hoping you see the Chinese way, then I ask. But I not have chance."

"I don't understand."

"I go to Hong Kong many years ago, and I go to China see the grave for my parents, but I not take my children." She hesitated. "Now, I come back China, need go see the grave for my parents. Have to do that."

"You mean like my father did?"

"We come here, I not know what to expect. I only talk to Uncle Chun-Kwok. I not want to tell you we see your father, because maybe . . ."

I peered at my mom. She had tried to protect me.

She said, "Your father meet us at airport, that the

surprise for me. At the restaurant, I not expect he ask you go to China."

"How did you feel about that?"

She glanced at me, then down.

"You didn't like it."

"Not that. Your father ask you go China, okay. But he ask you visit the grave for his parents . . ." She looked at me.

"You were going to ask me."

She didn't reply.

"I didn't know."

"I not say."

"Because my father asked first."

My mother nodded.

"Why didn't you tell me?"

"That not right way. You not see your father so many years." She stared at the concrete floor. "I take you away one time. You the man now. Not right for me stop you go with him."

I studied my mom. "Do you still want me to go to your hometown?"

Without looking at me, she gave a nod.

"Then we'll go."

Ingenuity 創造力

Chapter 23

I slept in the loft, and though it took getting used to, the low ceiling and enclosed space actually lulled me into a cozy sleep. My mother made do with the steel-framed foldout couch downstairs.

In the morning, I didn't want to shower in the filthy space posing as a bathroom, so I waited in line behind building residents to brush my teeth, wash my face, and dampen my hair.

My mom went later, and when she returned, her hair was wet.

I said, "You took a shower?"

"No. Really dirty in there, but I need wash my hair so I use bucket in the sink."

I helped her fold the bed back into a couch. "I still can't believe Cheun Chi and Mei Heng live here," I said.

"Better than nothing."

"What about that toilet?"

My mother broke into laughter. She continued to the point of hysterics, her whole body undulating in waves.

"What's so funny?"

"I guess you have to learn how to use."

"That's just hilarious. Go ahead, laugh. Just wait till you have to take a shower in that . . . that . . . shed!" I pointed toward the door.

My mom shrugged. "That what they have to do."

"How long do you think they'll stay here?"

"They not marry long. Maybe they save money and move another place."

"I thought the companies in China provide a house for you."

"That true, but Cheun Chi prob-ly want to be close by Wai Fong. Very easy for him and Mei Heng go there eat every day, because not far."

My mother toweled her hair. Amazing how people took things like hair dryers or automobiles for granted. For me, it was no big deal to drive a few blocks to the grocery store. Here, when I referred to my car, Mei Heng looked at me as if I had swindled her parents' life savings. No one in their family knew how to drive, and her expression indicated it wouldn't have been out of the question for them to go their entire lives without learning.

I fastened my travel belt around my waist, and Mom said, "Have to be very careful here."

"I know; it's more dangerous than Hong Kong, right?"

Her stare left no doubt. "Wai Fong tell me one night she very tired, fall asleep on bus, not long. She wake up and her purse gone. You know what they do?" My mother grabbed an imaginary strap at her shoulder and, with an abrupt motion, sliced it in two. "They take when she sleeping."

"Did she call the police?"

"What they can do? The robbers not stay there wait for police. I tell you another thing. Mei Heng walking on street one time"—my mom copied the woman's rapid-swaying hips to perfection—"carry the purse." She slung the towel onto her right shoulder. "They come take from her, run fast." In a single movement, she flung the towel across the room.

My mother continued, "You know what she say?" She

shot me a direct gaze. "Always have to carry purse like this." She traced a strap over her neck and diagonally across her body.

I patted the leather pouch. "At least we have traveler's checks."

"But have to be careful the passports. Also, we have the money your father and Number One give."

"What'd you do with that money, anyway?"

Her face beamed with the smile of a convict cruising past the prison gate in the laundry truck. She went to the refrigerator, opened it, and took out her purse.

"I pretty smart, hah?"

"Yeah, but what about going outside?"

My mom closed the refrigerator, contemplation creasing her brow. She sat on the couch, then whirled toward me. "I have good idea." She untied and removed one of her tennis shoes, reached into her purse, and pulled out the roll of Chinese notes. She inserted part of the stack into her shoe. My mother put her foot back in and stood, stomping down on her sole as if testing the fit before purchase. She fastened the laces and strode around the living room. "Not bad. They take the purse, no get money from me."

Mom sat and undid her other shoe. She slapped the mat next to her and said, "Come here and put in your shoe."

I unlaced my Reeboks, and a few minutes later, we both stood on a stash of Chinese currency.

* * *

My mom decided she and I would go to Beijing first, though she remained steadfast in referring to the capital as Peking. Wai Fong took us to travel agencies. Each time we talked to an agent, my mother went through a litany of

"

questions like a criminal investigator.

One tour was too expensive. Another didn't depart on the correct day. A third lasted too long. It made me glad we didn't have to go clothes shopping. I could imagine rummaging through thrift stores trying to find the right color, style, and size at 80 percent clearance. Wai Fong showed tremendous patience. She accompanied us all over town, and the two women kept a running conversation throughout.

My mom reported that Wai Fong knew the owner of a travel agency, but that he usually didn't go into the office until noon. Two more stops and we entered a grand hotel lobby boasting shimmering, wax-tiled floors and towering, cathedral ceilings. The hotel flaunted an elegant restaurant, bar, and even a bookstore off the lobby. Workers outfitted in white coats assisted an array of guests in fitted suits and cocktail dresses. I wasn't hopeful about the prospects for a reasonably priced tour here.

Wai Fong led us to a glistening green marble counter where she spoke to a stretched and balding fellow with a long neck, pointy nose, and squinty eyes. He looked like an ostrich in a burgundy coat. After a brief exchange the man shook his round head while responding to Wai Fong in a firm voice.

My mother entered the discussion, but he didn't waver. He answered every question in a calm and detached manner, maintaining a stony face.

Wai Fong put her hand on my mom's shoulder to stop the inquiries and made a request to the clerk. The man regarded her noncommittally and picked up his phone. He talked to someone briefly and, exuding the air of someone undertaking an enormous burden on our behalf, signaled us to follow him. Then he guided us through a nearby doorway past aisles of people busy behind steel desks. He stopped in front of wooden double doors and knocked.

A man came out and greeted Wai Fong with a hearty smile and handshake. This person, middle-aged, wore a three-piece suit and the demeanor of a corporate CEO. The ostrich-guy turned and headed toward the lobby.

Wai Fong introduced the CEO to my mother, who was so focused on the matter at hand, she forgot about me. Wai Fong relayed some information to him and motioned to us. My mom added her input in an impassioned display worthy of a closing argument before the Supreme Court.

The man listened with the focused impartiality of a trial judge, nodding and commenting. When he heard enough testimony, he held up his hands and rendered a verdict.

My mother fell silent, a good sign. If the decision had gone against her, she would've wasted no time appealing. The man led us back out to the lobby and gave an order to Mr. Ostrich, who now seemed much more accommodating.

Wai Fong thanked her friend and he departed.

Mr. Ostrich computed some figures and relayed a price. My mother hesitated. She whispered something to Wai Fong, who looked puzzled, but waited.

Mom spoke to me. "You still have money, right?"

"The traveler's checks?"

"No, the money from your father."

I looked down. "The money in my shoes?"

"They have good price for us go Peking here, but have to pay now. We should use money from your father for trip, so we not have to carry. What you think?"

Before I could respond, she said, "The man before, he the manager for travel agency. Wai Fong know him so he helping us. The trip we want all full, but he make okay for us go. He helping lots."

"So do we pay now?"

"I tell Wai Fong we should do in manager's office."

"We were just there."

"Have to or we take money out pay here."

I scanned the lavish surroundings and pictured us removing our shoes, standing on the sparkling, tiled floor in sweaty socks, and plunking the scuffed sneakers on the marble counter to make the purchase.

Wai Fong explained to Mr. Ostrich, who gazed at us in visible annoyance. He accompanied us to the manager's office again.

There, sitting on plush leather chairs, my mother and I took off our shoes and pulled out the perspiration-damp bills. The manager could only shake his head and smile as we plopped the moist notes onto his polished rosewood desk.

Divided 分裂

Chapter 24

My mother and I took a bus with Wai Fong, Cheun Chi, and Mei Heng, who had invited us to stay at her parents' home for the weekend while they vacationed. Wai Fong's husband did not accompany us. We rode in an old creaky coach that felt like a dilapidated school bus in dire need of new shocks. After forty-five jarring minutes we arrived at Foshan, a city west of Guangzhou known for dragon boat races, elaborately staged Chinese opera, and prominent examples of ancient Asian architecture.

We got off at a soaring residential high-rise, and Mei Heng led us through its neatly landscaped circular courtyard to a modern elevator. On the twelfth floor she directed us down a carpeted hallway to a door displaying a green plastic mat on the porch.

We entered a spacious living room with a hardwood floor. I saw functional furniture: high slope-backed couch and chairs without cushions, a short, curve-legged oval coffee table in front of the couch, brass lamps on matching end tables, and a twenty-inch TV on a stand with a rack of magazines underneath. A stainless steel Thermos and drinking glasses on a tray sat atop a bureau next to the TV. A wood-framed picture of wild horses galloping on an open plain hung on the wall. I could see part of the kitchen from the entrance and four doors down a hallway. Compared to Mei Heng's apartment, this was a penthouse suite.

Mei Heng guided me to a room equipped with a double platform bed. A small chest of drawers and a night stand with a clock and a lamp completed the furnishings.

She said, "You stay here."

Mei Heng seemed more abrupt with me over time. Whatever the reason, it made me uncomfortable, and I noticed myself distancing from her.

I put my travel bag on the mattress and thanked her. She nodded and left.

Later, my mother came into my room and told me Mei Heng had offered to take us to see some historical temples.

I hesitated. "Tell her thanks, but I'm tired. I'll just hang out here."

* * *

At dinner, Wai Fong prepared a meal of steamed rice, fried bok choy, chicken, and bitter melon soup. We ate at a square, Formica dining table against the wall in a kitchen that dwarfed the others I had seen in Hong Kong. Still, it was smaller than the one in my San Diego apartment. During a lull in the conversation, I said to Mei Heng, "Your parents have a nice house."

She continued to chew, then swallowed. Looking at me out of the corner of her eye, she said, "Okay, but maybe house, eh, more big in your country."

"It depends. I live in a one-bedroom apartment that's a lot smaller than this."

Surprise registered on her face. "But you have car?"

I hesitated because when I mentioned my car on the first night, she had unleashed a diatribe about American excess.

My mom broke in with a comment to Mei Heng. They talked, and soon, Wai Fong and Cheun Chi joined in. Their discussion diverted the topic, and I breathed a little easier.

In a while, Mei Heng said to me, "You speak, eh, good English."

I nodded. "Thanks."

"But you speak no Chinese?"

Her eyes stared straight into mine. I said, "Not much, no."

"Maybe hard for you, that." An accusing tone.

I spooned some sour soup with chunks of bitter melon into my mouth, chewed, swallowed. "It's not so hard. Everybody speaks English in America."

"Maybe hard if family Chinese."

She turned, reached for some bok choy, and spoke to Cheun Chi.

* * *

Late that night my mother and Wai Fong talked with Cheun Chi. I stepped into the kitchen for a glass of water and stopped in the living room. Mei Heng sat on the couch in an oversized T-shirt and baggy sweat pants, her legs crossed in a yoga position, watching a program about Hong Kong.

I decided to make one last attempt to be cordial. "That place is getting a lot of attention right now," I said.

With her narrow eyes still fixed on the screen, she bobbed her head and said, "Yes. We are very looking ahead to Hong Kong come back."

"The people here are excited about it?"

"You know, we go to Beijing, eh, two months ago. We see the watch, eh no . . . clock?" She hand-traced a large circle.

"That's right."

"But with the, eh, numbers to show how much the time

before when Hong Kong come back to us."

"A clock counting down the days?"

"Days, hours, eh, smaller."

"Minutes?"

"Yes, that."

"Do you have pictures?"

She turned and studied me. Then she hopped off the couch, went to the bureau, and retrieved a stack of film envelopes from a drawer. "Come. I let you see."

I sat near her on the couch and set my glass on a cork coaster on the coffee table as she thumbed through the envelopes. She glimpsed the first picture of each and rearranged the order of the piles.

"This the good one." She pulled out a set of photos and flipped through them. She showed me a picture of her on a huge stone structure besieged by a mass of people in the background. "Here, we are visit the Great Wall."

"Wow, I didn't know it was that high."

"Very big. We need to climb go up."

She handed me a photo of Cheun Chi on steep stone steps.

"It looks like a castle," I said.

She passed me another of the two of them in a guard tower on the Great Wall. The shot was off center, as if someone unfamiliar with the camera had snapped it.

"Is it really as long as people say?"

"Long." She spread her arms far apart. "You will go to Beijing this trip?"

"We're planning on it."

"Good. You see. You keep, eh, walking and walking and get tired, but it never stop."

More pictures of them there. The next envelope held

prints taken inside a military museum: Cheun Chi next to a huge tank emblazoned with a red star, Mei Heng in front of a rifle exhibit, another by a display of handguns, old Chinese military uniforms and helmets, hand grenades in a glass counter.

"A lot of weapons," I said.

"Oh, all the kinds. Cheun Chi like to see the guns, so he like this place."

"Where is this?"

"Close by the Tiananmen Square."

"You went there?"

"Yes, is the famous place. You go, you will see too."

I remained quiet for a moment, wondering if I should ask about the tragedy. Would the people here even acknowledge it?

"Did you know about the student demonstrations there?"

"Everybody know about that. The very bad thing. Many days on the TV."

"Really?"

"Yes, the news show, eh, many days."

"So you know what happened?"

She nodded. "That the really bad thing. I was watch the TV night, eh, June, four"—she held up four fingers— "nineteen eighty-nine. Many students at Tiananmen. They yell loud, say the bad things about the gov-ment. More yell and scream. Then TV go off."

"You turned the TV off?"

"No, by self. Everybody the TV go off. Nobody see after that."

"They shut off the broadcast?"

She nodded.

"So people didn't see what happened?"

"We do know. Everybody know that the bad thing." She shook her head slowly.

"You know students were killed?"

She nodded. "The gov-ment give them the chance, tell them go home, but they do not listen. The gov-ment send the train for them, eh, pay for that. But they keep stay, not listen, make bad, so the soldiers have to shoot."

I stared at Mei Heng in disbelief—her grim face, eyes stony and remorseless; her expression conveyed regret at an ugly but necessary action.

Mei Heng was my age. She worked, had gone to school, and knew English. She was married to the son of my mother's oldest friend. Had my mom stayed in China, my life probably would not have been too different from Mei Heng's. Still, I couldn't imagine justifying the slaughter of unarmed students. How could Mei Heng be blinded by this kind of denial? Did other Chinese people feel the same way?

And how to respond? In my heart, I knew the massacre was wrong. But could I say so? She invited us to stay at this house as her guests. Her mother-in-law pulled strings to help us find a tour of Beijing. We were in her country.

But how could I remain silent? Those young people gave their lives for their beliefs—the right to protest, democracy, freedom of speech—principles that founded our country.

"Mei Heng, I have to tell you that I see it differently. Those students didn't do anything wrong," I said.

She gazed at me with a hard-edged focus.

I continued, "They were just voicing their beliefs. They weren't hurting anyone. In the US, we feel that if something is wrong, you speak out. And you work to change it. That's very important to us and it's something we've always supported."

She stayed silent for a moment. Then she said, "We know your country strong. You have the big army. But why you try hurt us? Maybe you have the army, but we have that too. You have guns, we have. You have ships, we have too. Maybe you are big, eh, but we are not afraid." She glared at me, her eyes striking like bayonets.

"Wait a minute. What do you mean we try to hurt you?"

"Your country help Taiwan. You give the guns and, eh, ships for them. Why your country do that? Taiwan part of China. The people Chinese. They should come back to us. Soon, Hong Kong come back. Taiwan, too. But your country try to stop this, help them."

Was that how people in China saw us? Street bullies attempting to dictate the policies of other nations by a show of brute force? How to argue? Had we not supported Taiwan? And did we not sell ships to them? Neither a politician nor diplomat, I found myself in the uncomfortable position of defending our country's foreign policy.

"In the past, we have seen Taiwan as more independent than China. When we see countries that are trying to be free and self-governing, we help."

"Then you make hard for us."

I stared at Mei Heng for a long time. She regarded me with the kind of look I used to get from the American kids at school. Only now it came from Chinese eyes.

Consequences 後果

Chapter 25

Wai Fong took us to the airport in Guangzhou where my mother and I departed to Beijing. After a three-hour flight we landed and met up with our tour group. When the guide spoke, I realized my mother had booked a Chinese tour to save money.

Our group entered a bus to take us to our hotel. Beijing was different from other parts of China. Practically spotless streets posed a sharp contrast to the litter-ravaged roads in Guangzhou and Shenzhen. I saw modern houses and buildings, unlike the squalor of decaying tenements and shops in the major cities to the south.

I gazed through the window to observe the cyclists in their own bike lanes. Helmetless riders in business suits and formal leather shoes carried everything from packages to briefcases in metal baskets attached to their handlebars. In America they would've been taken for Mormons.

Pedestrians, many dressed as if going to church, strode the sidewalks. No low-rider shorts, pierced body parts, or visible tattoos. Nor any Mohawk and step haircuts, or bright purple and lime-green streaks along the scalp. It made me wonder how this society would've embraced a Dennis Rodman.

The driver took us through a section of dense multistoried office buildings. He turned into the parking lot of a large hotel and the tour guide delivered a serious message.

My mother listened intently and said, "Wow. Have to be very careful."

"Don't tell me, it's even more dangerous than Guangzhou, right?"

"No. He say no can throw trash on street here, against the law. Lots policemen. If they see you doing that, will give ticket. Have to pay money for that."

"The police are watching for litterbugs?"

"That what he say. No can put cigarette on the street, have to use trash can. Even no can spit on sidewalk."

"You can't spit?"

"Have to use Kleenex and throw in trash."

"You're kidding."

"No kidding. Be careful or have to pay money for that."

"It wasn't like that in Guangzhou or Shenzhen."

"This different." She lowered her voice. "This the capital, so many people come from other countries to see. The Communists want to look good for that."

There were similar ordinances in San Diego, but nobody took them seriously. I never heard of anyone cited for littering. Here the law seemed to be no laughing matter.

The guide directed us into the lobby of the hotel and conveyed more information. People formed a line at the counter before he finished speaking.

We positioned ourselves behind a woman and her little girl, then set our bags down. The woman turned and asked my mother a question that led to a lengthy conversation. In time my mom introduced me to Sok Wai and her six-year-old daughter, Mui Ying. The two women continued to talk with the unbridled enthusiasm of teens at a slumber party.

I looked around at the modest hotel—small lobby, two

elevators opposite the entrance, and a tiny snack shop at one wing. Workers wheeled laundry carts down a narrow hallway past the elevators.

A woman's loud voice drew my attention to the lobby counter. I recognized the mother with her little boy from the plane; she was now in a heated argument with the desk clerk.

He extended keys to her, but she shook her head as if he offered a mousetrap for her room. She yelled at him and the employee dropped the keys on the counter in a gesture of unmitigated exasperation.

Hands out in a conciliatory manner, our guide tried to intervene.

Sok Wai commented to my mom, who nodded and gave a brief response.

I asked my mother about the commotion.

She said, "The woman upset because she pay for five-star hotel. This one only three star. She say she get gypped off about that."

"This is a three-star hotel?"

"You look around, can tell. This not really high-class place."

"Is that what we paid for?"

"I not know about that. More important how expensive and what days we go."

The dispute continued at length. Then the irate woman snatched the keys off the counter, called to her son, and stomped off to the elevator.

My mom and Sok Wai resumed their conversation as we lugged our bags forward. A boy of about ten, in a Chicago Bulls tank top brandishing the number 23, came up to question my mother.

Her reply prompted him to ask more. She said to me, "He want to know why we speaking English, so I tell him we from America."

I looked at him and said, "Hi." He stepped back and quickly retreated to his place in line.

"Prob-ly he not get chance to see too many Americans."

* * *

My mom surveyed our room. "Not fancy, but is okay."

It was far from extravagant: bathroom with shower and sitting toilet, plastic hangers in a coat closet, a flimsy dresser, and single beds separated by a nightstand with an ashtray and telephone on top. "That woman in the lobby was pretty upset," I said.

"She the good-looking woman, prob-ly get used to everybody treat her like queen."

"The woman in line really took to you."

"Her name Sok Wai." My mother went to the bed by the window, pressed the mattress with her hand, then sat. "Maybe she not know anybody here, so she not want to be all by herself."

"She's touring Beijing with her daughter?"

"She say her husband working, busy all the time, so he pay for her go. I not know, but I get feeling something not right for them."

"What do you mean?"

"She not sound happy talking about him. And she tell me a lot, so maybe she need somebody talk to. Maybe I wrong, but I get feeling."

Although my mom qualified the statement, her tone indicated an unwavering certainty.

I sat on the bed closest to the door. In a moment, I said,

"You think Wai Fong's ever been here?"

"She not get to travel much. She always working and her husband not like to travel."

"That man was weird. He had some kind of a complex about food. He kept telling me to eat, even if I was full."

"He older, so supposed to tell you what to do. Wai Fong do like that too. It mean they like you."

"How was it for you to see Wai Fong again?"

"I not see her since I run away from China, so we talking a lot."

I paused. "Was it hard for you to come back?"

"It okay. I see how people living here. . . . It make me think about my life before in China. And Hong Kong too."

"Do you ever think about my father?"

She nodded.

"How was it for you to visit his family in Chashan?"

"Not bad. They friendly, asking lots questions about you. I expect that, because this first time they see you."

"It wasn't hard to be there with them?"

"Maybe little bit." She hesitated. "The pictures, that uncomfor-ble for me."

"You didn't have to do that."

"They not try do the bad thing. They want most the pictures for you. But they ask me take with your father." She stared at the floor. "It make me think how they see us. Maybe they just taking pictures, but I think they still see us like the family when they do that."

My mother's quiet voice communicated sadness and regret.

I regarded my mom. I was learning so much about her on this trip. Yet there were still many things I didn't know about her past, her family, her relationship with my father.

"Do you ever think about what might have been if you had stayed in Hong Kong with my father?"

She started to say something and stopped herself. Then she directed a gaze that told me she thought about it often, something she couldn't help doing, and that the question would haunt her for the rest of her life.

Wall 牆

Our heated bus climbed the steep, mountainous road to the Great Wall. A misty fog blanketed the area in gloomy gray, and the thick haze camouflaging the surrounding trees was enough to send goose bumps up my arms as neither my mom nor I brought jackets. As we drew closer to our destination, I saw numerous vehicles loaded with people.

The first glimpses of the ancient stone structure brought "Oohs" and gasps from our fellow passengers. Huge, the Wall came out of the fog like a monstrous serpent from the water. The shrouded atmosphere prevented us from seeing its length in the distance, but the barrier stretched upward like an ancient fortress.

Winding, bumpy roads led to a village courtyard teeming with tourists carrying Great Wall T-shirts, brass replicas, and other mementos purchased from merchants using stacked cardboard boxes to prop their displays.

Our driver parked the bus and we all got off. I wore a polo shirt and shorts, and the chilly air nipped at my bare arms and legs. Mom's short-sleeved blouse and polyester slacks couldn't have provided much warmth. The tour guide broke into a lecture, but I wanted to get moving to generate some body heat.

I scanned the immense, foreboding structure looming a hundred yards from us. Lines of sightseers climbed the steps to the interior like ants on a kitchen counter. After the guide finished speaking, our group started forward.

My mother reported, "He say we can go anywhere around, but have to meet here in three hours."

My watch read 11:14 a.m. China time. "Okay, so we'll have to be back at two."

"Make sure not forget." A moment later, she said, "It cold here."

"I guess we'll just have to keep moving; either that or buy souvenir sweatshirts."

Her sour expression indicated my idea held about as much appeal as hitchhiking back to the hotel. Only in a dire emergency would she condone purchasing something so frivolous, and frostbite didn't qualify.

At the foot of the Great Wall our group separated. My mom and I climbed the stone steps among a flock of people. At the top, twenty-five feet up, we gazed out at the dense trees and sweeping mountains. I could see the mist-engulfed courtyard in the foreground where the bus dropped us off.

We walked along the length of the Wall, stopping to take pictures at one of the many cavernous watchtowers. The interior, made of dark stone blocks, approximated the width of two cars. At various intervals, sharp-rising steps conformed to an elevated portion of the sloping landscape.

We paused after climbing one of the steeper sections. Between labored breaths, my mother said, "The man say they build this by hand. They make from the ground before Chee-ses born, over thousand miles long. But it falling apart, so have to make again, use rock."

I shook my head. "Imagine how many workers it must've taken."

"The king order for that; people have to go. Some, they take from village, never come back."

Not my idea of a dream job: leaving my family to construct a stone barrier at the outskirts of nowhere, slaving for years on end, never to see the completed fruits of my labor, and as a final reward, a multitude of back ailments culminating in an early demise from herniated disks or ruptured spines. Without a doubt they could've used some serious labor negotiations.

My mom added, "In China, that the way. Everybody have to work hard."

I regarded her, a woman who personified hard work. She managed her own real estate properties in San Diego, and even after she sold her restaurant, she stayed on at the owner's request to help run the business. "How long do you think you'll continue at the restaurant?"

Bewilderment flashed in her eyes. "No can tell about future. Sometimes, things change. Never know."

"Since you don't own it anymore, you probably won't work there long, right?"

"The work not bad," she said. "Now Roger no have job, so we need somebody make money."

I looked at her and saw a woman who had been doing just that—whatever was needed—her entire life.

"What do you think you would do if you weren't working there?"

"I do many jobs before."

"No, I'm not talking about earning money. I mean what would you enjoy?"

She laughed. "I no can be doctor or lawyer, because I not have education. Some people go school, can sit office, type computer, but I no can do. I not go school, so for me, no choice, have to work hard."

We moved slowly through the crowd. Then my mother

said, "What about you. You have master's degree. You keep helping the people in school?"

"For now. I still need to get my license. Maybe eventually I'll open up a private practice for marriage and family counseling."

"You have own business, people come to you fix the problems?"

"Something like that."

"You think enough customers for that?"

"As long as people have problems."

"You help families and kids too?"

I nodded.

"But if you not married and not have kids, how you can help them?"

"Well . . . ah . . . I don't necessarily think you have to be married or have children to counsel families. I have a lot of education and training. That's what's important."

She studied me. "For me, if I take plane go somewhere, I want pilot fly the plane before."

We had been on the Wall about twenty minutes. Mom gazed ahead at the fog-shrouded hills. "Look the same to me if we keep going. Nothing to see."

Leave it to my mother to be completely unimpressed by mankind's greatest structural achievement. We turned, and after a few minutes, we passed a young couple posing at a watchtower in matching, oversized Great Wall T-shirts. The man draped his arm around the woman's shoulder as a bystander lined up the shot. My mother said, "You going out with Vietnam-nese girl how long?"

"Six months."

"She nice?"

"I guess so." I could feel my discomfort growing.

"You get along good?"

"Okay."

"What she like?"

"Why do you ask?"

"You go out six months, I not know about her. If Michael have girlfriend, he tell me. I know if Renee dating someone, but you different. I never know the things about you." My mom looked away as she said this.

I hesitated. "I guess I never thought it was that important. We're friends. You haven't met a lot of my friends."

"That not the reason."

"What do you mean?"

"I get the feeling you not want to tell me about her."

She was right. I had always kept my mother at a distance. But why? Protection. From? Judgments. Expectations.

And . . . like a faint beacon, the answer flickered from the hidden depths of my being. Truths. Painful truths. About people. About myself. My silence kept me safe—and separate.

I began slowly. "Sometimes, you have your own agenda about things. Like you have my life all mapped out. It's hard because I don't know whether I'm living my life for me or for you." I forced myself to take a breath. "All my life, I've tried to meet other people's expectations. The kids in school used to tease me for being Chinese. No matter how hard I tried, I could never be Roger's son. Donna wanted me to be the kind of father she needed for her children." A strickened pause. "And I had to be successful to please you. I just never felt that being me was good enough."

Neither of us spoke. My mom studied me with hurt in her eyes. Then I saw something else, something genuine and unshakable. Understanding. And a beginning. She looked at me, not in the way a mother would observe a child, but with the wonder, and sadness, of a parent seeing a son, now grown, embarking on his own life.

Hate 恨

Chapter 27

I stood in the hotel room gazing out the sliding glass
window at the frenetic activity in the street below.

My mother's voice rang out from across the room. "Boy,
they not do good job cleaning here today. The cup for brush
the teeth still the same. They not change that."

I turned to see her come out from the bathroom in
pajamas with a damp blouse and pants draped on hangers.
She hung them in the closet.

I said, "You think those will be dry by the time you need
to wear them again?"

"Will be. You see."

Mom walked to her bed. She threw back the thin spread,
sat, and inspected the sheet tucked into the mattress. "And
you see this?" She pinched at something on the pillow and
held it up for me. "See? This my hair. That mean they not
change the sheets, you believe that? They just make the bed
and go."

"Maybe they were in a hurry today."

She shook her head. "In Peking, hotel, restaurant,
everything run by government. Government job, nobody can
fire you, so they not do good work."

"Does that include the tour we're on?"

"Sure! You see the restaurant they taking us for dinner?"
She scrunched her face. "Food lousy. Vegetables cook too
long, not the good flavor. And not much meat. We already

191

pay for, so they taking us to cheap restaurant make more money for them."

My mother leaned toward me as if to convey a secret with national security implications. "I tell you something. The man and the driver, they drop us off at restaurant, then come back pick us up later. Must be they go eat somewhere else."

I walked over to my bed. "They do this all the time, so they probably get sick of eating the same food. Come to think of it, they must get tired of seeing the same sights over and over again. I know that going to the zoo or Sea World every week would get old real quick."

"But that the job, so they need do."

I flung myself on the mattress. It felt like landing on a trampoline. I sat up and looked at the phone on the nightstand. "Hey, you think I can call San Diego from here?"

"Who you call?"

"I was thinking about Quyen."

"Long distance, another country, you know. Costs lots money for that."

"It won't be long. I just want to tell her everything's okay."

She scooted toward the phone. "Let me see, I think the tour man say we have to tell worker before make the long-distance call." She picked up the receiver, listened, and pushed a number.

My mom spoke briefly, hung up, and handed the receiver to me. "Have to push oh, oh, one for English line for long distance."

I entered it. A recorded female voice, in broken English and barely audible on a static-filled line, told me my call couldn't be connected. I hung up and tried again.

"What wrong?"

"I don't know. I'm getting a recording."

"You use oh, oh, one?"

"Yeah. I did it twice."

"Let me try." I passed her the phone. She made an attempt, then looked at me and shrugged. "Not working. You want me go down to lobby, find out what wrong?"

"You'd have to change first. Don't worry about it."

"You sure?"

I nodded.

She put the phone on the nightstand. "You must be really like this girl, hah?"

"What, just 'cause I'm trying to make a call?"

"Must be if you try from China."

* * *

In the hotel cafeteria I couldn't stomach much of the rice soup and cold rolls the hotel always served for breakfast. Instead I amused myself by performing a math "mind reading" trick for a trio of teens from our tour: a hyper-expressive boy with an infectious smile named Hon Hung who spoke some English, his contemplative cousin, Lok Him, and a bookish girl named Yen Liu the two boys had met on the tour.

My magician friend, Henry, from elementary school had shown me the trick. He would have me pick a number in my head and, without my divulging it, run me through a series of arithmetic steps. Then he would hesitate a moment with a set of fingers pressing into his temples and call out the number I had arrived at. The day he revealed the secret, I must've gone through a hundred sequences trying to find one that didn't work. The trick never failed.

Hon Hung begged me to show him the solution, but

I just smiled. He kept at me throughout the breakfast,
and by the time we boarded the bus, he even attempted
to bribe me with money. I reminded him that I lived in
America, a land of incalculable wealth. His face was a study
in disappointment as we made our way to the back of the
coach.

He and Lok Him took seats in front of my mother and
me. Yen Liu and her aunt sat across the aisle from them. As
we started forward Hon Hung turned and asked me about
America.

I said, "How about if you give me your impressions first?"
Hon Hung looked confused.

"Tell me what you think about the US."

He consulted his cousin and both nodded. Hong Hun
said, "US rich, many cars." His eyes grew big, as if to mimic
the vastness of our perceived wealth. "Drive fast."

I laughed. "That's probably true compared to China.
What else?"

He paused, then pointed at me in the manner of a
game show contestant with the answer to the million-dollar
question. "Many guns. Ah . . . shoot, kill. Ah . . . steal the
money."

I looked at my mom and she shrugged.

I turned to Hon Hung and said, "You think we have a lot
of crime?"

"Yes. US, many guns."

"Tell me more."

"US have much sexy, no clothes."

It was beginning to sound as if he had taken in too many
James Bond flicks.

"How do you know all this about America?"

He paused and spoke Chinese to my mother.

She said, "He watching American movies and listen to music."

Sylvester Stallone and Madonna were educating other countries about our nation's culture. Lok Him spoke and this prompted a question from my mom. Yen Liu responded.

My mother reported, "They say US number one powerful country. They agree about that, but they say we little bit selfish. They say US have big army, many guns and ships, so try to scare everybody. They say we helping Taiwan so that show we selfish."

For the second time in a week a Chinese person mentioned America's involvement in Taiwan—a definite bruise in China's consciousness.

"I don't know the ins and outs about Taiwan. I only know we were trying to help people," I said.

My mom conveyed this. The youths' restrained nods indicated they heard, but didn't necessarily agree.

Lok Him commented.

My mother said, "He think America hate China. He ask if that true."

Hate? That's how they thought Americans viewed them? It seemed preposterous. Yet prior to this trip, I equated China with Communism and authoritarianism. Tiananmen Square. A government and people who couldn't be trusted.

I regarded the three teens and said, "Hate is a really strong word, and I wouldn't use it to describe the differences between our two countries. Maybe we just don't know each other very well."

* * *

Our driver let us off at an expansive cement courtyard surrounded by prominent government buildings. At one end, across a busy street, I saw a gigantic marvel of ancient Chinese architecture. An imperial palace crowned with a sloping, two-tiered, golden-tiled roof stood in majestic dominion over the entire area. Below the roof, ten evenly spaced, royal-red pillars framed a series of vertical windows decorated in gold trim. A thirty-foot-high protective wall in front displayed a huge picture of Chairman Mao Zedong between two long banners of white Chinese characters.

The tour leader informed us we were in Tiananmen Square, that Chairman Mao proclaimed the People's Republic of China here in 1949. My mother translated his presentation: established in 1651 at the transition between the Ming and Qing dynasties, enlarged in 1958 after the formation of the People's Republic, the literal translation, "Gate of Heavenly Peace." It seemed the cruelest of ironies.

The enormous courtyard could hold a million people. Walking across, I pictured it in 1989, an early summer morning filled with young, idealistic, Chinese students protesting in the name of freedom and democracy.

A chill shot through my body, and I shuddered at images of armed soldiers marching toward the square, firing into the surrounding mass of demonstrators, wounding and killing.

Screams. Panic. People running blindly. Hysterically. Unable to get away. Blood-soaked cement. More gunfire. Loud. Rapid. More screaming. Bodies crumpling to the pavement. But not just bodies. People. Young college students with families. Spouses and loved ones. And children.

A single haunting question knifed into my thoughts: How could they do that to their own people?

The rest of the day dissolved into a blur. My mom told

me we visited the Chairman Mao Mausoleum, the Museum
of Chinese History, and a military exhibit.

I didn't remember. The images from Tiananmen Square
kept flooding my mind.

That night in the hotel room, I lay on my bed.

My mother said, "Raymond, you okay?"

"What? Yeah . . . Why?"

"You quiet."

"I was just thinking." After a silence, I said, "What did
you think of today?"

A pause. "We see lot, walking too much. When we go that
place for Mao Zedong, how they keeping his body, make me
feel strange."

"They really worship him here."

"Look like in China, he the great man. Everywhere go,
have pictures for him. All I know is my family happy before,
have the good life."

I recalled her story. How the Communists murdered her
father, imprisoned her mother, and forced a twelve-year-old
girl to flee from her family. Why? For what possible reason?

Lok Him's question crept into my mind, resonating with
greater and greater force. Did the US hate China? Did the
Communists hate my mom's family?

How could they? They didn't even know them. Then
why? My mother's parents had money and property. If one
family could possess wealth, wouldn't others want that too?

And if a band of renegade students was allowed to
protest for democracy, wouldn't others soon follow?

Threat. Fear. That explained how the Communists could
rip a family apart, one that had done them no harm. How
a country could fire on its own people. How we could lock
our own citizens of Japanese descent in internment camps

during World War II. How our soldiers could take part in the My Lai massacre in Vietnam. How Nazi Germany could murder over six million Jews.

And if people and nations continued to destroy what they were afraid of, that which they didn't understand, what would become of us?

Rage 憤怒

Chapter 28

The bus driver dropped us off at a bustling shopping district in the heart of Beijing. My mom and I walked with Sok Wai and Mui Ying, the woman and her daughter my mother befriended in the hotel line the first day of our tour. Pedestrians packed the sidewalks next to an array of modern department stores boasting shiny glass displays and multiple floors of merchandise.

Sok Wai stopped at a women's shoe store, while Mui Ying kept tugging at the strap of her mom's purse. Sok Wai reprimanded her and continued to browse.

My mother and I wandered ahead to the window of a teashop displaying an assortment of boxed teas from China. We stopped there to wait for Sok Wai and Mui Ying. My mom said, "Sok Wai have the hard time now. She and husband getting divorce soon."

"Really? Why's that?"

She shook her head. "Her husband want son really bad. When Mui Ying born, he disappointed about that. In China, only supposed to have one kid, but he have to have son. The husband very successful in business, so they pay lots money for government, let them try again. But they have another girl."

"You buy the right to have a second child?"

"After first one, have to pay. In China too many people, so government not want you have kids. You see? We in China almost two weeks, not see one woman carry the baby in stomach."

True. I hadn't seen a pregnant woman in any of the Chinese cities: Shenzhen, Chashan, Guangzhou, and now, Beijing.

"So what does that have to do with their divorce?"

"Her husband get upset. He say waste the money have another girl. Because he successful, lots women chasing him, say will have son with him. So he have boy with another woman. He supporting the other family now."

"You're kidding."

"No kidding. He leaving Sok Wai to marry the woman with boy." She shook her head again. "Sometimes I really not understand Chinese people."

"She told you all this?"

"Sure."

"So what's she going to do?"

"Prob-ly go Hong Kong, marry somebody there."

"Just like that?"

"That what she say."

"And the children?"

"She taking the young one go. And husband taking Mui Ying. That why Mui Ying come this trip, so can be with Sok Wai before go with husband. Maybe they not see each other again."

A final trip between mother and daughter. Did Mui Ying know? It struck me as absolute insanity for the girl to lose her mom just because her father wanted a son.

Sok Wai strolled toward us holding her daughter's hand. The girl's little innocent, button eyes gazed about as she followed her mother's lead. Sok Wai clutched a bag full of shoe boxes in her other hand.

I offered to carry Sok Wai's package and she smiled, but shook her head. My mom spoke to her and Sok Wai looked at me and nodded. I took the bag and strode behind Sok Wai and her daughter, watching them go down the sidewalk together.

* * *

On the last day of our tour my mother and I ate another round of the hard rolls and bland rice soup at the hotel cafeteria for breakfast. The place's star rating dropped at least two notches in my book with culinary fare that made me long for hospital food.

Neither my mom nor I ate much. We carried our bags out to the bus and took seats when the tour guide rushed aboard and dashed through the aisle to my mother. He communicated in an urgent manner.

She said to me, "We have to go back to hotel. He say something wrong."

"What do you mean something's wrong?"

"I not know, but have to go."

The man led us off the bus, across the lot, and into the lobby. He pointed to a woman at the counter whose face seemed almost too narrow to prop up her wide, black, horned-rimmed eyeglasses. When my mom approached, the woman reported something and handed her an invoice. My mother disregarded it, shook her head, and responded in a tone of heightened irritation.

An argument ensued, their voices rising with each exchange. The woman kept gesturing at the slip. My mom continued to shake her head and pointed to the elevator.

Then the woman picked up the phone on the counter, punched some numbers, and spoke into the receiver. My mother didn't let up while this clerk talked on the phone.

I went to the counter and said, "What's going on?"

My mom looked at me with angry disbelief in her eyes. "She crazy, say we owe money for long-distance phone calls. She try to show me day and time we make."

"We didn't make any long-distance calls."

"That the night you try call your girlfriend."

"But I didn't get through."

"That what I tell her, but she keeping say we make three calls, have to pay. I tell her we not going to pay for that, so she getting the boss."

"How much are they saying we owe?"

A disgusted sneer formed on her face. "Three hundred dollars Chinese."

Forty American dollars. "That's ridiculous!"

"That what I say." She whirled and launched some seething words at the woman, who issued an icy reply. This sparked another barrage.

A tub of a man with bloated cheeks and a bulging lower lip came down the hall and joined the fracas. My mother paused as he conferred with the desk clerk. The man—his girth taxing a plaid jacket—picked up the invoice from the counter, scanned it quickly, and rendered his decision. My mom shook her head in defiance and the supervisor engaged her in a replay of the earlier confrontation. The gaunt-faced woman appeared relieved to let him assume the battle.

My mother and the new combatant went at it. I watched my mom: eyes riveted, tendons bulging in her neck, head lurching forward with the fury of each verbal volley. I had never seen her this bitter, this intense, even in the worst fights with my stepfather. Sheer unrelenting hatred rained from her words, as if she were attacking someone who had done something heinous and unspeakable to her.

At that moment I realized it wasn't the money. My mom wasn't just mad or upset. I heard anger in her voice, but more than that, I could feel her frantic desperation. Her anguish and horror. She was yelling as if her very life depended on it, as if the man in front of her had stolen something treasured and sacred.

Then I saw it in her eyes, the frightened eyes of a twelve-year-old girl, watching, helpless, as soldiers took her mother and father away.

And now she was venting her rage at this man, the supervisor, a person in charge, a symbol of China. Like a child who never had the chance.

I stepped slowly to my mom and put my hand on her shoulder. She turned and I saw the traces of terror on her face. In as calm a voice as I could muster, I said, "Mom, it's my fault. I'll pay the money."

She stared at me a moment before recognition came to her eyes and her face changed, as if her darkest enemy had transformed into her son.

She didn't say anything. But in that brief instant I caught a glimpse of it, stark and raw. Grief.

She managed a blank nod.

I unzipped my belt pouch, removed two twenty-dollar traveler's checks, signed them, and put them on the counter.

I went to my mom, placed my hand on her arm, and guided her out to the bus.

Connection 投緣

Chapter 29

Wai Fong's husband, Sung Bok, met my mom and me at the airport in Guangzhou and we took a taxi to his house. There, he insisted we eat a lunch of steamed rice, wok-fried scallops, and black mushrooms. After the meal my mother conversed at length with Wai Fong, and her sour tone told me she was relating the telephone incident in the Beijing hotel.

In the midst of a spirited dialogue between the two women, Sung Bok motioned for me to follow him. He directed me into the kitchen to a wall phone, picked up the receiver, and dialed. He spoke to someone, and in a moment, he handed the phone to me. An operator with a thick Chinese accent requested my needs. I thanked Sung Bok, who nodded and returned to the living room. I placed the call to the United States.

I glanced at my watch and determined it was 1 a.m. in San Diego. I prayed for Quyen or her younger brother, Phong, to answer.

Three rings and I recognized her mother's groggy voice. I asked apologetically to speak to Quyen. Relief swept over me when her mom sounded pleased to hear my voice. She told me to wait.

"Ray?" Quyen's whisper brought another twinge of guilt.

"Hi, Quyen. I'm sorry to call so late."

"You better be." She laughed. "Don't worry. Phong's

friends are always calling at all hours of the evening. So where are you?"

"I'm at a friend of my mom's in China. We're in a city called Guangzhou. They let me use the phone but I don't want to tie up their line too long. I just wanted to say hi."

"Hi, Ray, so how's your trip?"

"I can't begin to describe it, Quyen. I have so much to tell you, but not on the phone."

"Did you see your father?"

"Yeah. I did."

"And?"

"It went okay."

"Tell me, Ray!"

"I will, I promise." I paused, then asked, "How are things going for you there?"

"Oh . . . okay."

"I guess I deserved that."

"You tell me, I tell you."

"I'll tell you everything—when I see you."

"Promise?"

"I swear." I hesitated a moment. "Hey, Quyen. I, uh . . . kinda miss you."

She didn't hesitate. "I miss you too."

"Listen, I better get going."

"Wait. I pick you up on Wednesday, right?"

"Is that okay?"

"What if I said no?"

"I wouldn't believe you."

"Then I guess it's okay."

"I really appreciate it, Quyen. Hey, tell your parents I said hi."

"Oh . . . thank you, Ray." The surprise registered in her

tone. "Say hi to your mom and dad for us too."

After we said good-bye, I hung up and gazed at the phone.

*   *   *

When I returned to the living room my mother stopped her conversation in midsentence and said to me, "How it go? You get through?"

"Yeah, she was glad to hear from me."

"That good. I talking to Sung Bok. Tomorrow, we taking taxi to my hometown, okay?"

I nodded. "I'm ready."

Reverence 尊敬

Chapter 30

The rain grew heavier as we passed countless empty fields on the two-lane road. In the cab's backseat next to my mom, I listened to the hypnotic sweep of the windshield wipers.

I said, "How are you going to know where the graves are?"

"My brother hire the man before taking care the graves. I call the man from Wai Fong's house, tell him we come today. He going to take us go."

For a time no one spoke. Then Mom pointed to the driver and said, "He very nice. He smoking, but I ask him yesterday not to smoke when we in the taxi. You see? He not have one cigarette since he picking us up."

I looked at the driver's reflection in the rearview, the deep haggard pouches under his eyes that gave the appearance of someone in dire need of strong coffee. "How is it that he can take us on this kind of a trip?"

"We pay five hundred dollars Chinese. Taxi cheap in China, not like Hong Kong, so he very happy take us go."

This man was delighted to rent his services for the entire day in exchange for sixty American dollars. We approached a desolate intersection and the driver questioned my mother, who gave a brief reply.

I said to her, "What's the name of the city?"

"Tai Shan, but not city. Very small."

We drove toward a lone farmhouse surrounded by crop fields and barbed wire, and I saw a man, wearing a straw hat and drenched work clothes, pedaling a bicycle at the side of the road with pant legs rolled up to his knees.

Pockets of pine trees emerged against a mountainous backdrop and wild brush and grass thickened the terrain. The mud-coated road was bumpy, entire sections in desperate need of repair, and I prayed that we wouldn't have to make a sudden stop, picturing us sliding off the shoulder and careening into the adjacent ditch.

Suddenly, my mom said, "I think that the place."

She pointed at a gray-brick house in an open field, and I recognized the evenly divided fish ponds bordering the house, but I didn't see a driveway. My mother spoke to the driver, who braked onto the grassy shoulder. He honked his horn, then again.

A man in a clear rain slicker came out of the house and waved to us. He jogged through the field and over the wet road to enter the front seat. The dark-complexioned man, probably in his fifties, turned to greet my mom and communicated clipped sentences in a hoarse voice as if talking posed a hardship. His serious eyes protruded from narrow sockets and his teeth jutted forward at an extreme angle, giving his face a pinched, nervous appearance.

The driver pulled us onto the road again. A half mile up the man directed the driver to stop on the shoulder and stepped out into a burst of rain. My mother reached for her umbrella and opened the cab door to a pelting deluge, so I slid across the seat and readied my umbrella to follow. The driver popped the trunk and my mom and I retrieved the supply bags. When we joined the man in the slicker, he extended his hand for my mother's package, and she relinquished it to take one of mine.

Our guide waded through knee-high grass to a narrow trail and we tracked him up the steep and muddy path through grass, rocks, and dense brush. The man kept wiping his eyes with his palm as water trickled from the hood of his slicker and my mom tapped him on the shoulder to offer her umbrella. He nodded and took it, and she scooted under mine.

We pushed forward against the wind and whipping rain until we came to a four-foot-wide ravine blocking our path with rushing water. The man spoke to my mother, then proceeded into a river that completely covered his work boots and soaked his pants to the knees. My mom marched across, seemingly oblivious to the current washing over her tennis shoes and pants, and I trekked behind her, my lower legs immersed.

On the other side of the ravine, I could feel the squishing of cold, wet socks inside my sneakers and the bottoms of my soggy jeans clinging to my skin. More hiking. My arms throbbed from holding the bag and an umbrella that leaked water onto my shirt and my mother's blouse. We came to a clearing overlooking a valley of pine trees. Then I saw it—a small cement slab on the sloping bank ahead.

We made our way there. No pillars supporting a protective overhang, no cement foundation, no shiny letters embedded in polished granite, just a simple headstone inundated in grass and weeds.

My mom dropped her bag and hurried to the foot of the headstone to pull at the plant growth with her bare hands. I set my bag and umbrella down to help. We cleared the entire area around the gravesite as if our very lives hinged on it. My mother was soaked, her hair dripping moisture onto her face.

She wiped the sleeve of her blouse against her forehead and went to get her bag. She carried it to the headstone and removed a container of roast duck. I gathered my umbrella to shield my mom from the rain, and the guide brought the remaining bags.

My mother opened the box of pastries, put it on an empty sack, and rotated it toward the headstone as if positioning a dinner setting for an honored guest. She placed apples, mangoes, and plums on another bag. After arranging the food, she took out the incense sticks and planted them in the ground near the fruit, dug out a box of matches, and struck one against the side of the box. It didn't light, so I bent lower to protect her from the gusting wind. It took three attempts to produce a flame and she held her free hand around the flickering glow like a child cupping a butterfly. Carefully, my mom brought the match to the incense sticks and the sweet smell of jasmine wove into the air on thin curls of smoke.

Rain swept over us. Drops ran down her neck as my mother knelt at the headstone, put her hands together, and bowed three times. She closed her eyes and spoke Chinese in a quiet, solemn voice as if conveying something from the depths of her soul. She continued for a time, and I watched, transfixed.

My mom repeated the bows before opening her eyes. They were red and moist, and I knew the drops trailing down her cheeks were tears.

She stood, moved to the headstone, and placed her hand on it in a silent, private communion. Then she turned and walked slowly toward the edge of the clearing.

I went to where my mom had been, knelt, and propped

the umbrella over the food and incense. I put my hands together, closed my eyes, and bowed three times. As I prayed, images appeared: my mom as a peach-faced, ponytailed little girl playing in front of a spacious brick house; her mother, wearing the traditional black tunic top and pants, the long, loose sleeves rolled up to the elbow as she scrubbed clothes by hand in a basin with a wooden washboard; her father, slender like me, with silvering hair, working the fields with a hoe, raking and tilling the soil. I could see them as clearly as a rainbow along a majestic sky. I observed them prior to the fateful day the Communists came, before their lives were changed forever.

I spoke in a soft voice. "My name is Raymond and I'm your grandson. I'm sorry it's taken me so long to come here.

"I live in America and it's important that you know I have a college education. My mom worked hard to give me that chance.

"Sometimes, I don't realize how lucky I am, the opportunities I've been given. I take things for granted—my schooling, my job, my family.

"But on this trip I've seen how hard people work, the way they live. It's helped me to appreciate my life in America and that's something I'll never take for granted again."

I paused, drew a deep breath. "There's something else I want you to know. It's about my mom. She brought me here today to be with you. It was important to her.

"She's had a hard life. I didn't know how hard until this trip. That was my fault. For so many years I didn't want to be Chinese. I didn't want to be different, so I never asked about you. I never wanted to know.

"I'm sorry. It was wrong and I ask your forgiveness.

"Your daughter has cared for a deeply wounded man, a

man who couldn't love her, but she stayed with him and tried to help him.

"She raised two sons and a daughter, often by herself. Michael and I are very different. He's practical and business-minded like she is. Someday, he's going to run his own marketing firm and he'll be successful. He learned from my mom.

"Renee is close to Mom and that's good because Mom needs someone to confide in, someone who will be there for her.

"Me, I'm stubborn. Mom would call it hardheaded, and she'd be right. But if there's one thing I know, it's that I'm going to make a difference in this world. Maybe with my work. Or my writing. Or the kind of person I am.

"My mom raised me to be a man of integrity and honesty, a man who cares about others. She taught me courage by the way she's lived her life.

"I want you to know these things about your daughter and I hope that you're as proud of her as I am."

I bowed three times, opened my eyes, and peered at my grandparents' headstone. Then I stood, turned, and joined my mom.

Home 家

Chapter 31

The ashen clouds released a light rain. We dropped off the guide at his house and the taxi driver took us into Tai Shan, my mom's hometown.

No one spoke as the cab squeezed through the channel of roads so narrow they couldn't have been built for cars. I saw old and battered houses: moldy walls of cracked, discolored brick, rows of empty clotheslines dangling from splintering, wooden shafts, and worn pails and wicker baskets heaped near grimy gullies.

Our driver pulled to a stop as the road dwindled into little more than a bikeway scrunched between decaying buildings. He turned and spoke to my mother, who responded with a nod. He shut off the engine, and she and I got out.

I held the umbrella above us as my mom and I walked the dirt path between tattered one-story houses. I didn't see yards or fences, just a lone step at the foot of a weathered front door, one after another, a line of faceless homes.

My mother gazed at the surroundings as if in a trance. She stopped at an abandoned gray-brick building that loomed above the others. A muddy, barren courtyard led us to the base of a fifteen-foot-high entrance. The door had been removed, and a set of four, inlayed, black Chinese characters in two columns of cement framed the opening. We entered.

The deserted house comprised one level, with walls of

broken bricks extending upward twenty feet. I counted three windows consisting of two-foot-square sections carved out of the brick. A portion of the collapsed ceiling left a pile of debris on the ravaged, faded stone floor.

My mom stepped across the room and touched her hand to the wall. "This the house my family live. My father build." Sadness tinged her voice.

I nodded. A long silence. Then I asked, "What do you remember?"

An empty smile crept onto her face. "We very happy before. My father, he own the land, grow rice and vegetables."

Her gaze traced the bare walls, up along the ruptured ceiling, down to the caked rubble on the floor, exploring every nook and contour of her house. And in her eyes, I witnessed a gentle transformation. Her whole face took on a softer sheen, a window of vulnerability, as if she were journeying back to a place of timeless innocence.

She spoke, and even the tone in her voice sounded younger. "My father, he not only grow food. He very smart. Because the test he take, the government give him important job. I not know how to say, but he go to meetings, talking, and make the decisions.

"Sometimes he take me go to town with him." She smiled and her face beamed with the radiance of a child after performing her first cartwheel. "Lots people come shake his hand, and they give him basket for food. Everywhere he go, people give the fish, vegetables, and rice." She put items in a basket only she could see. "They not want him pay."

She continued, "And they come from many towns, ask his advice. For Chinese people, the name very important. My father smart, so they want him help name the baby. He glad to do that."

"People respected him."

She nodded.

I remained quiet for a few moments. Then I said, "What about your mother? What did she do?"

"Before, the woman no can have job, so she taking care the house. But she work very hard, cook, clean, and she taking care for me." My mom paused as if to bask in the warmth of a cherished memory. "She always tell the funny stories, making me laugh." My mom smiled again, and I could see her as a little girl, giggling with her mother. "She very good, much younger than my father, because she the second wife for him."

"What happened to his first wife?"

"I not sure. She die, some kind sickness. My father spend many years by himself, so he want to get marry again. My mother come from poor family, but that not important to him." She drew a deep breath, released it. "When she ask him help her family, he give the money for them. She say she lucky find man do that, but I think my father the one lucky find woman, work hard and care about her family too."

She studied the house again like a treasured painting. After a while she slowly turned and walked out the door into the courtyard. I took a long look at the house, bathing myself in its essence, then followed her.

The rain had eased, and a rooted, vibrant freshness scented the air. In the courtyard my mom stared at the rain-soaked earth. "When Wai Fong and I little, we played here." She spoke in a subdued voice. "Not much candy those days, so we make own snacks." A faint smile. "We get the sweet potatoes and dried squid, come out here to cook."

"Here?"

She nodded. "We get the bricks to put." Her hands

demonstrated. "We use sticks and grass and light the match, put the sweet potatoes and dried squid. We turn with stick, and when done, we cut and eat."

"Did you play with Wai Fong a lot?"

"Sure. We play hide-and-seek, games, many things. She one year older than me, but we the best friend."

I marveled at the image, because until this trip, I had only seen my mom as a stern, relentless, wealth-driven woman.

She turned to look back at the house. I moved beside her and followed the line of her gaze. "What do those Chinese characters say?" I asked.

"My father make when he build the house. It mean . . . like the tree, when it grow, come from one." She extended her open palms together, as if to receive a precious gift. "Come from one, but when grow, the branches go out." She spread her arms upward. "But still always one." She clasped her hands together. "The family like that."

* * *

That evening at Wai Fong's house, we shared a meal with her family. Sung Bok warmed the roast duck and chicken we had taken to the gravesite, and we celebrated my grandparents' memory with a home-cooked feast.

My mother stayed up late into the night, talking to her best friend. As they reminisced I saw it in my mind, clearer than a San Diego summer day, the two of them—young girls in the courtyard in front of my mom's house—sharing childhood secrets while cooking sweet potatoes over a shimmering fire.

Confession 告白

On the train back to Hong Kong, my mother gazed out the window at the veil of cloud cover. An attendant served refreshments and my mom took a sip from her cup of Coke. She turned to me and said, "Raymond, something I need tell you."

It reminded me of her preface before rendering the account of her vicious mugging in Hong Kong at the start of our trip. I recalled my guilt at having been unable to feel for her.

Now my mother peered into my eyes. "I try tell you before, but I not know right way. That night your father buy us dinner, I almost tell you, but . . ."

My mom's candid tone conveyed the importance of what she was about to say. She gathered a breath that seemed to reach down to the inner recesses of her being. She drank from her cup. "Long time ago, when you and me leaving Hong Kong—" An extended pause. "Your father not know we not going back."

"What?"

She looked down. "I try tell your father I not happy, but when I say I need talk to him, he always say later. Then he go out. We not see each other much, never talking. I think he know something wrong."

"I don't understand."

"We very poor. He lose job, so I working hard support

us. Maybe he feel bad about that. He just go out drink, that what he do. If something wrong, he not say. He do like that. So I do like that, too."

"So what did you tell him?"

"What I can do? Your father not happy, I not happy. Then I almost get killed. What I can do?"

"You didn't tell him?"

She didn't say anything.

"Mom?"

"After what happen to my mother, father, I want go far away from China. I go Hong Kong, but I not happy. I want go America. Some people tell me easier to go with no kid, but I say no can do. I have to bring you. I tell your father I take you go America, but who know what going to happen? We not know if we can stay there. Maybe we have to go back or maybe he think we come back for him."

She shook her head slowly and continued. "After I meet Roger, I want to write your father, but so many things . . . I not know what going to happen. When Roger and I get marry, I try to write, but I not know how to say. How you tell your husband you marry another man? How you tell him you take go his son?"

She stared at the metal armrest between us.

I sunk into my seat. My heart was pounding, a dozen thoughts funneling inside my head at once. My father . . . My mother . . . All these years . . . No wonder . . . Suddenly, amidst the swirling chaos, a thread of reason emerged. "Mom, you've got to tell him that you remarried."

My words appeared to jar her. She steeled her eyes on me. "He must be know by now. All these years, I not see him. He know."

"But you still have to tell him. If you don't, you'll carry it for the rest of your life."

Without answering, she turned to the window.

Farewell 告別

Chapter 32

On our last night in Hong Kong, Aunt Poi Yee cooked a dinner for everyone: her family, my father, Hoy and his family, Number Seven and his entourage, and my mom and me. We brought stools and three folding tables from next door. It took some doing to squeeze everyone into the tiny living room, but we somehow managed.

My father, beside me and quiet as usual, appeared content to be with his family. I tapped him on the shoulder and gestured to his bowl. He looked at me, and a thin smile tugged at the edges of his lips. He brought some rice and black mushrooms into his mouth with his chopsticks.

Hoy said something to me in his loud and distinct voice, and the mirthful gleam in his eyes told me to be wary. My mother's response elicited ringing laughter at the table. A discussion followed, including comments from most everyone on a topic that must've held great fascination for them.

I felt uneasy hearing my Chinese name mentioned. In time my mom said to me, "They want to know when you coming back to Hong Kong. I tell them cost lots money for that, so maybe when you get marry, we come again."

"What!?"

She shrugged.

Hoy spoke, and Uncle Chun-Kwok, my father, and Number Seven chimed in.

My mother said, "When you marry, they want you have another wedding in Hong Kong. They also give you one in China. They pay for that."

I was speechless.

* * *

My father met us at the airport the next day. At the security checkpoint, my mom and I thanked Uncle Number Six and his family, then bid them a heartfelt farewell.

I approached my father. We embraced. I took hold of his hands and said, "*Dojeh*."

His eyes shone.

My mother faced my father, hesitating an instant before going to him. She grasped his arm and directed him to a private area. She spoke and he nodded. He pointed to me and she glanced over. They continued to talk. Soon she reached for his hand, held it, and looked into his eyes. He nodded again. She released his hand and they returned.

Then my mom and I walked to our plane.

Epilogue 結語

I married Quyen in 1998 and visited Hong Kong again to introduce her to my father. When Quyen and I had kids, I heard through my mom that he wanted to see our children. So I invited my father to the US, told him I would pay for his plane ticket and he could stay with us. I never received a response. It made me think of all the years he never contacted me. I didn't think he cared.

In March 2010, my father suffered a stroke and died. It was my family's obligation to go to Hong Kong to take part in the funeral. I was his only child; my kids were his only grandchildren. Once there, Uncle Chun-Kwok brought my father's possessions to me. From a faded, leather carrying bag, my uncle took out a small, tarnished brass picture frame holding a photo of Quyen and me at our wedding reception. My father kept the picture on his nightstand beside his bed. It was his favorite.

Then my uncle handed me a worn, crusty plain brown packaging envelope that contained photographs and cards my mom had sent throughout the years. There were pictures of me in my high school cap and gown, Quyen and me at a formal dinner while dating, the two of us beaming at our wedding reception, our son Kevin on his third birthday, a five-month-old Kristie cradled in my left arm on the couch. I found Christmas cards from my mother nestled between the photos, and a neatly folded paper with a hand-drawn heart and a message of love from Kristie.

I leafed through more pictures and discovered a group shot of my father, mother, and me next to a number of relatives and friends on a pier in Hong Kong. I must've been four at the time. I came upon another photo of me in elementary school, maybe eight years old and wearing a gaudy blue sweater. My father had kept every item relating to me and my family.

My uncle said my father never traveled. In his seventy-six years of life, my father had never been on an airplane.

For most of my life, I didn't think my father cared about me. As I looked at the pictures of my family with tears in my eyes, I knew I was wrong.

Acknowledgements

The journey I took to Hong Kong and mainland China in 1996 changed my life. I met a father and discovered a mom. The trip opened my eyes to a relationship with Quyen and showed me how to be part of a family.

I started working on an autobiographical novel after returning to San Diego. I had only written short fiction and a few journalistic pieces before that, but this particular story seemed to channel out of me onto the page over the next year. I woke up every morning and followed the narrator on a journey that allowed me to experience Hong Kong and mainland China once again.

After revising and sharpening the novel for many years, I sent it to literary agents and collected a batch of rejections. Then in 2006, I submitted the manuscript to an agent who liked my work and asked if the events were based on real life because the story read like a memoir. I admitted my novel stemmed from personal experience, and the agent suggested making it a memoir. The decision was mine. I combed through every passage to ensure the truth was depicted on the page. I checked the chronology of scenes with a journal I had kept of my trip and consulted with my mother to gauge the accuracy of my recall. I changed the names of some people in the book to safeguard their identities, but I am satisfied that this memoir is conveying my experience.

The agent and I were not able to place the manuscript

with a publisher, so I began researching and submitting to independent presses on my own. I encountered rejection after rejection, but finally, a Florida publisher offered me a contract in 2011—fifteen years after my trip and countless hours of writing and revising. My dream had been realized; the memoir would be out in 2013.

Then on July 11, 2012, I received an e-mail from the publisher with the subject line "Unfortunate news." The owner was closing her company at the end of the year for personal reasons. My memoir had been slated for 2013, but she would not be able to publish it after all. My book rights reverted to me, and I needed to find another publisher. I was devastated.

I was studying creative writing in a MFA program at Antioch University Los Angeles at the time, and my mentor, Bernadette Murphy, supported me during that difficult period. She encouraged me to start submitting again, and I did.

I'd like to say I found another publisher right away, but I endured a number of rejections before discovering Apprentice House. I admired how this university press used real-world experiences to teach students book publishing. They actually acquired, developed, and produced their own titles, and I would be contributing to the education of future industry publishers.

I wanted to share this story because it has been a long and arduous path to publication, a road filled with detours and disappointments, but the journey has been worth it.

A few notes about the memoir: the story is based on real experiences, and I haven't created composite characters in this book. For the romanized Cantonese terms, I used *A Practical English-Chinese Pronouncing Dictionary* by

Janey Chen, published by the Charles E. Tuttle Company (1970) and *English-Cantonese Dictionary: Cantonese in Yale Romanization*, published by New Asia — Yale-in-China Chinese Language Center, the Chinese University of Hong Kong (1991). My daughter, Kristie, who is studying Mandarin Chinese at Riverview Elementary School in San Diego, researched the Chinese characters for the chapter headings. Her first Chinese teacher, Grace Cox (Wang Lao Shi), checked our usage of Chinese characters.

Excerpts from this book have appeared in other publications. "Reverence" was published in *City Works 2006* and as "China" in *Chicken Soup for the Soul: Thanks Mom* in 2009. The epilogue ran in *USA Today* as "In Death, Assumptions About Dad Melt Away" on June 18, 2010. I changed the title of "China" to "Foreign" for the Spring/ Summer 2014 issue of *Small Print Magazine*. The chapters "Hate" and "Rage" are combined into the story "Hate" for the Fall 2014 issue of *Segue*. I want to express my gratitude to Jim Miller, D'ette Corona, Glen Nishimura, Steve Brannon, and Eric Melbye for publishing these excerpts.

The publication of a first book is the realization of a writer's dream, and there are many people who have supported me. I want to thank Jim and Carol Hillegas, Ron Symons Jr., Sal Flor, Gerry Vanderpot, Lance Soukhaseum, Robert Scott, and Rosemarie Robinson for their friendship; Susan Hasegawa, Karen Lim, Judy Patacsil, Aileen Gum, Elisabeth Newbold, Brenna Ring, Jennifer Geran, Carol Withers, George Tubon, Aaron Raz Link, Angela La Voie, and Allie Marini Batts for their encouragement; Glenda Richter for igniting the literary flame; Ashley Geist for stoking the passion; and Paul Lapolla for believing in me.

The following writers provided invaluable feedback,

guidance, and information: Adrian (Dick) Magnuson, Erin Grady, Richard Lederer, Nina Romano, Barbara McMikle, Laurel Corona, Leonard Novarro, Rosalynn Carmen, Gloria Tierney, Kelli Turpin, Andromeda Romano-Lax, Alix Moore, and Barbara Morrison.

It has been a privilege to learn from the MFA faculty and students of Antioch University Los Angeles, and I am grateful to the mentors and workshop leaders who have shown me why words matter: Steve Heller, Peter Selgin, Sharman Apt Russell, Bernadette Murphy, Christine Hale, Terry Wolverton, Brad Kessler, and Erin Aubry Kaplan.

It has been an honor to be an Antioch MFA graduate, and I feel blessed to have befriended Angela Franklin, Julie LeMay, Christine Buckley, Rana McCole, T.G. LaFredo, Wendy Fontaine, Jennifer Koiter, Rachael Warecki, Allison Lynn, Tanya Ko-Hong, Daniel Reinhold, Breawna Eaton, Lise Quintana, and so many others who believe in the cause of social justice.

I also need to acknowledge my employer, San Diego City College, for making it possible for me to attend Antioch.

Kudos to Katherine Pickett for her editorial skills, Vina Rathakoune for creating a fabulous cover in collaboration with the Apprentice House design team, Charles Cuthrell for an extraordinary book design, and Kevin Atticks for his patience and astute guidance.

I cannot go without mentioning the outstanding staff and students at Apprentice House for making dreams come true.

Most of all, I want to thank my wife, Quyen, who lights up my world, and my children, Kevin and Kristie, for inspiring me each and every day.

* * *

Postscript: I am about to send my manuscript to Apprentice House to begin the process of producing a book. At the same time, my stepfather, Roger Uhlenkamp, is suffering from the final stages of colon cancer, a condition he is not expected to survive. Roger and I have never been close, but he helped to raise me, and there is one thing I will always remember about him. He taught me how to ride my first bike when I was eight. He ran behind me as I pedaled my green Huffy Stingray up and down Cisco Street in China Lake, California. He held me up on that bike until I could ride it on my own.

About the Author

Raymond M. Wong is grateful to live in San Diego with his wife, Quyen, and two children, Kevin and Kristie. He has served as an assistant editor of creative nonfiction on *Lunch Ticket*, Antioch University LA's literary journal. In addition to his MFA in Creative Writing from Antioch, he holds the Master of Science degree in Counseling from San Diego State University. He works as a counselor at San Diego City College and volunteers with his children to deliver meals to homebound elderly through Meals on Wheels in El Cajon.

Wong knows the pain and emptiness of being an outsider, and he does workshops and speaking engagements in the community to share his experience, to reach out and connect with others who feel alone and alienated. He found acceptance, forgiveness, and a sense of purpose through writing.

I'm Not Chinese: The Journey from Resentment to Reverence is his first full-length book, and he is currently writing another book about the father he never knew.

View the author's reading of "Reverence" on YouTube: http://www.youtube.com/watch?v=aIVT5pLTihA.

Visit his website www.raymondmwong.com

Apprentice House is the country's only campus-based, student-staffed book publishing company. Directed by professors and industry professionals, it is a nonprofit activity of the Communication Department at Loyola University Maryland.

Using state-of-the-art technology and an experiential learning model of education, Apprentice House publishes books in untraditional ways. This dual responsibility as publishers and educators creates an unprecedented collaborative environment among faculty and students, while teaching tomorrow's editors, designers, and marketers.

Outside of class, progress on book projects is carried forth by the AH Book Publishing Club, a co-curricular campus organization supported by Loyola University Maryland's Office of Student Activities.

Eclectic and provocative, Apprentice House titles intend to entertain as well as spark dialogue on a variety of topics. Financial contributions to sustain the press's work are welcomed. Contributions are tax deductible to the fullest extent allowed by the IRS.

To learn more about Apprentice House books or to obtain submission guidelines, please visit www.apprenticehouse.com.

Apprentice House
Communication Department
Loyola University Maryland
4501 N. Charles Street
Baltimore, MD 21210
Ph: 410-617-5265 • Fax: 410-617-2198
info@apprenticehouse.com • www.apprenticehouse.com